GREEN HOPES

I am grateful to Maryvonne Yvon and Francine Comte for their help and patience in the preparation of this book.

GREEN HOPES

The Future of Political Ecology

Alain Lipietz

Translated by
Malcolm Slater

Polity Press

English translation © Polity Press 1995
First published in France as *Vert espérance: L'avenir de l'écologie politique*
© Éditions La Découverte, Paris, 1993.

This translation first published in 1995 by Polity Press in association with
Blackwell Publishers Ltd.

Published with the assistance of the French Ministry of Culture.

2 4 6 8 10 7 5 3 1

Editorial office:
Polity Press
65 Bridge Street
Cambridge CB2 1UR, UK

Marketing and production:
Blackwell Publishers Ltd
108 Cowley Road
Oxford OX4 1JF, UK

Blackwell Publishers Inc.
238 Main Street
Cambridge, MA 02142, USA

ISBN 0 7456 1325 X
ISBN 0 7456 1327 6 (pbk)

A CIP catalogue record for this book is available from the British Library and
the Library of Congress.

Typeset in 11 on 13 pt Times
by Best-set Typesetter Ltd, Hong Kong.
Printed in Great Britain by T.J. Press, Padstow, Cornwall

This book is printed on acid-free paper.

In memory of Renée Conan

Contents

Preface

To a Left-Wing Friend Still Hesitating to Join the Ecologists

This could have been the title of this book. There are in fact many ways of coming to ecology – through love of the beauty of flowers, the splendour of deserts, the calm of the country-side or the disturbing profusion of tropical forests, through the grace and tranquil otherness of wild fauna. Or else through rejection of sexual roles which enclose human tenderness in the brutality of relationships based on relative strength, which hound deviant behaviour, which stop fathers having deeply loving relationships with their children; through the search for a new way of living with others, on an everyday level. In my own case, it was revolt against an unjust economic order which tears society apart between rich and poor, defiles nature because it has no respect for human dignity, ravages continents because it exploits the work of men and women enslaved by their conquerors.

Like many others, I came to Green through Red – I came to ecology because of disillusionment with the Left. I had believed in this tremendous hope passed down from generation to generation, from the Spartacus rebellion, the peas-

ants led by Münzer, the sansculottes of Babeuf and the silk
workers of Lyons, down to the Paris Commune, the workers'
soviets of Petrograd and Berlin, the guerrilla warriors of
Cuba's Sierra Maestra and the resistance of the Vietnamese
people.

It is many years since I had to accept the obvious – that this
elevated hope of the human heart was not realized under the
banner of socialism, through the idea of collective ownership
which would end social distinctions. It is not enough to lay
the blame on the 'deviations' of traitors, of which there were
many: those who took the easy option and, once in power,
assumed the mantle of the existing order instead of trying to
change it. From reformulation to renewal and revolutions
within the revolution, it has to be admitted that socialism is
not the earthly manifestation of this dream which humanity
has in its head and which only has to be experienced (and
applied) for the world to possess it in reality. Human societies are infinitely more complex than socialism had believed. The dream of utopian communists in the nineteenth
century, of a community of individuals in free association,
delivered from the division of labour, fishermen in the morn-
ing, artisans in the afternoon and literary critics in the
evening – this dream will always be mine as well. History,
however, is an experimental science, and the communist
experiment is the tragedy of the twentieth century.

It is many years since I stopped identifying with the socialist or communist ideal, with the continuity (reconstituted,
recomposed . . .) of 'the Left', with the centrality of the
workers' movement. This identity, this continuity, this centrality are no longer mine. They are doubtless no longer
really recognized, in their heart of hearts, by most of those
who in France want to 'change things'. The reverence they

still have for the 'Left' identity is rather, I think, a sign of a certain honesty – of people who do not follow the crowd, but keep faith with what they were. They are faithful to, and heartened by, a combat whose nobility transcends the terrifying mess into which it is now sunk, along with 'socialism in action', not only socialist hope, but all hope. I respect this honesty, but it is only common sense to say again that one does not indulge in politics, or in critical theory, on the basis of childhood memories. Today's young people, coming to politics after the death of Mao and Che Guevara, have known nothing of socialist hope other than the 'socialism in action' of Brezhnev, or the management approach of the Mitterrand years. There *is* a movement which dreams of changing things, but to persist in calling this 'socialism' or 'communism' is simply to go no further than a circle of old chums. 'Old friends are what count', as the Georges Brassens song goes, but then 'our own gang, that's the rule' and we cling to it. This does not amount to a 'social movement . . .'

There is no need to remind ourselves why Marxism, historically constituted as the thought of communism, is no longer able to express aspiration for change. There have been many issues of journals devoted wholly to this question. Marxism, in a thought framework, in an organizing principle, in a very powerful version of what can be called a 'paradigm' (a word which will be used a lot in this book), encapsulated the target, the subject and the aims of the movement itself. *Anti-capitalist, proletarian, communist* – the movement was explicitly all three together. Let us add (and this was a grave mistake) that the unity of the party and the central position of the state ensured the unity of the three elements when they showed signs of separating. Also, underpinning everything, was the 'socialization of productive forces'.

We no longer believe in the unity of oppression: machismo, nationalism and productivism do not necessarily stem from capitalism. We no longer believe in the unity (or even the centrality) of the proletarian as subject. We no longer believe either in the New Jerusalem of communism. We are afraid of the all-powerful state. We are particularly afraid of the growth of productive forces.

Who are 'we'? Most of us are heirs of a Left which is without a heritage. So, what is there still left of the Red, other than the sombre glory of Spartacus, of Thomas Münzer, of Gracchus Babeuf and Rosa Luxemburg? It is perhaps a shame that these people no longer appear on our political banners: banners are another necessary element in politics, though clearly a reductive fervour and faith in heroes and saints can lead, in a complex world, to the worst monstrosities.

Those who no longer sing to Red tunes (except, as I have said and still say, among old friends and comrades), how can they indulge in politics at the present time? There were attempts at opening 'second fronts' alongside 'the main confrontation' between labour and capital. These included feminism and ecology itself, in its original guise of 'quality of life', but they were subordinated to the 'main' struggle, and this reduced their potential for change. The next stage, in the period from the 1970s to the 1980s in Europe and the United States, was the 'rainbow' approach – a mix of historical subjects (workers, women, small farmers, young people, homosexuals, ecologists, peoples of the Third World and so on), each fighting against a particular oppression, yet all needing to get together against something, in favour of something else. This was already a considerable step forward, and it led to the rise of alternative forces in Europe (the 'Grünen') and the Americas (Jesse Jackson's 'Rainbow Coalition', and the Workers' Party in Brazil), with or without the old icons. It was probably better for them if they did have icons, even if inappropriate ones, such as the Castroism of the Workers' Party of Luis Inacio da Silva ('Lula') and Chico Mendes, and if possible new ones, such as the Green of German alternative groups.

However, this postmodern cobbling together had its limits. This is evident above all in the discreet silence about contradictions *between* social movements. The workers' movement has never been either feminist or ecologist. Social contradictions did not run parallel, so social movements were not necessarily convergent. This convergence was to be a *social production* – the creation of a new paradigm, the unfurling of a new political banner.

I am now convinced that political ecology *can* be this new paradigm, this framework of thinking to unite hopes, the Green of the new banner. People will say (at least those who are honest enough to admit that Greens are not just concerned about cormorants caught in oil slicks) that Green is not a paradigm but an umbrella, a catch-all banner, a catch-rainbow device. But at least political ecology *is* trying to construct a paradigm, comparable in structure to the Red one. It is doing this by basing itself solidly on a material reality, by being against an 'existing state of affairs' (productivism and so on) which it tries to analyse in order to put up a better fight against it; and it has a value system (solidarity, autonomy, ecological responsibility, democracy) which expresses the hope of oppressed people. It also has a project already sketched out, that of ecodevelopment and sustainable development. The contrast with the Red approach is glaringly obvious: the adversary is many-faceted, shapeless, and is present in everyone's head; the subject is diffuse, complex, beset by contradictions; the aim is a problematic way forward rather than a New Jerusalem reached by going through the gates of revolution.

Everything still needs to be done, to be defined, to be constructed. I appeal to my friends who are moving away from the Red: rather than pursuing the idle dream of changing the Red, or remaining on the periphery in a tiny Red and Green grouping (Red through faith, Green through realism), I believe that the authentic way to keep faith with the struggles of the oppressed is to press ahead, together with ecologists, with that part of the Green paradigm which emphasizes a social and world-scale approach.

This book has come to fruition through the permanent dialogue that I have had over the last few years with people who were 'still' Red and Pink and those who were 'already' Green. Some of the ideas contained in it have already been aired in French journals and weeklies. My thanks go to those in charge of these publications and of the many meetings where these ideas took shape. My loving gratitude goes also to Francine Comte, my companion on this journey which has been both arduous and exhilarating.

PART I

Old Imperatives, New Hopes

1

Ecology without Consciousness is Body without Soul

Do ecologists need consciousness? I ponder this question every time I write a tract, brochure or book about political ecology. Some people (both friends and opponents of political ecology) think I have nothing to worry about. Ecology is a science; and scientists are certain that if we continue as we are, the results will be catastrophic – worsening greenhouse effect, disappearing ozone layer, less and less fresh water, more and more rubbish. *So . . .*

So what? Is it enough to be 'conscious' of problems in order to act 'to the best of one's knowledge'? Rousseau's meaning of 'consciousness' was different: '[We need] consciousness in order to love Good, reason in order to know it, freedom in order to choose it.' Freedom to choose is a matter of political struggle; using reason in order to know is a matter of scientific ecology. Between them, however, lies the problem of 'consciousness' – that which makes us indignant about something, and spurs us to action.

Fine, but action for what, or for whom? Rousseau's answer was ingenuous: for good, the good which was that of his age, conceptualized as 'morality', an amorphous secularization of the Judaeo-Christian heritage of 'Thou shall not kill' and the like. Our age has a different idea of good: it is self-interest. This is the ultimate form of Rousseau's ossification of Judaeo-Christian values. 'Thou shalt not kill', because that would be breaking the social contract which guarantees that others will not kill you, rob you and so on: 'Do unto others as you would be done by', 'Act so that your maxim becomes a universal one.'

This is where the problem arises: political ecology raises problems not amenable to any social contract or basic pact between free individuals. Thou shalt not kill whom? 'Thy neighbour', say Christians. 'Your partners in the social contract', say non-believers. Very good, but what about wild species? 'Nature was given to humanity', reply both Christians and secular productivists, of whom Luc Ferry, in his attack on ecologists, is a most recent example.[1] And what of future generations? Here there is disagreement. 'I don't care what happens after I'm gone', says the individualist who bases morality on 'self-interest'. If there is no interest expressed, there is no social contract. St Paul was more subtle: 'If the dead do not rise, let us eat, drink and be merry, for tomorrow we die.' In other words, I am prepared to be responsible for future generations on condition that, one day, we all rise from the dead. On this judgement day, I will be brought to account for not having cared for the heritage of future generations. But if the soul is not immortal, then I owe nothing to future generations. Let us eat our fill as we wish.

Those who do not believe that the soul is immortal can always apply Kant's consistency principle: 'Do unto others what they have done to you.' But all that previous generations have done for us is to have developed productive forces. We derive our comforts from their depredation of nature as they found it; we can therefore do to others who come after us what others in the past have done to us. Let us eat, drink and . . . In other words, the approach of 'immanence', of simple reason, of logic, in no way commits us to act.

The approach of 'transcendence', of the God of Judgement Day, could well be attractive if this God exists; but we must remember that in the Ten Commandments there was nothing about other species or future generations, just as there was nothing about slavery or the oppression of women: centuries of revolt were needed for groups of 'others' to assert themselves. 'Future generations' will embark on these struggles – but too late.

Nevertheless there is the feeling that what is lacking between ecological reason and ecological politics is a 'thou shalt not kill'-type link, a principle (or several principles) transcendent, but immanent in appearance. A perspective based on general interest, but elevated, far above species, genera and centuries. Thou shalt not trigger the greenhouse effect, because we know that life (of which thou art merely an atom) emerged and stabilized within the current temperature range, that civilizations developed within the even narrower confines of the present interglacial age, that human beings spread over the Earth as a function of temperature, and that if they were forced to flee by cyclones and deserts there would be bloody confrontations. In order not to trigger the greenhouse effect, refrain from doing anything, or do things with deliberation, restraint and respect.

But, says the Westerner, is this outlook not that of the East? Zen? Buddhist chanting? Yes and no. The elevated perspective, that of *Time become old*, is certainly that of Krishna in the *Mahabharata*. Krishna, however, sees war and self-destruction as the great river of life regulating itself. Both doing something and not doing anything are without significance. The Whole will triumph through the chance meeting of large numbers of erring individuals.

This is where an ill-assimilated East sets a fearsome trap for Westerners' guilty conscience, and in particular for ecologists: in the name of a 'higher consciousness', we may be tempted not to transcend the boundaries of instrumental rationality and respect for neighbours, but, on the contrary, to *retreat* from the moral imperative of the responsibility of 'humankind as demiurge', which knows full well that each of its acts influences the fate of the whole. This trap is nowadays seen in the *myth of Gaia* – Earth as an immortal goddess, persevering in her existence by driving mad those who try to ruin her. Certain aspects of 'deep ecology' are in danger of falling into this trap.

From this 'orientalism' which reduces the sense of responsibility, Judaeo-Christian and Muslim consciousness and the consciousness of individual responsibility were able to offer an escape route different from Kant's consistency or Rousseau's social contract: the broadening dynamic of altruistic personal consciousness. Dostoyevsky's phrase, 'We are all accountable for everything to everybody, myself particularly', is nowadays taken up by Emmanuel Levinas as the basis of his *think of 'the other'* approach. The problem, once again, is that 'everything' and 'everybody' have a wider scope for ecologists than they had for Dostoyevsky.

Combining the oriental 'everything' and Dostoyevsky's 'myself particularly' is doubtless the Great Vehicle of a morality for the twenty-first century; but thinking this morality, sharing it and, even more, putting it into practice, is another thing entirely! In this book, I will try to combine reasoned knowledge of the real world, which the ecological approach promotes, and the 'morality for our time' as constituted by the values of ecologists, in order to define a policy – in fact, mainly an economic policy, since I myself am an economist.

What are these values?

Solidarity: rejecting the exclusion of certain individuals, of a social category or group of countries. It is not just 'equality of opportunity', but a matter of each person being given opportunities at all times.

Autonomy: where in factory, countryside or office (for individuals), in its own territory (for each community), there is the possibility of 'seeing where one's own acts are leading', being in control of the consequences (and, if possible, the conditions) of one's activities.

Ecological responsibility: not just being 'need-oriented' (we are aware of how needs can be manipulated), but sometimes limiting one's own needs, and always choosing the means to fulfil them which take account of the interests of life on our planet and the rights of future generations.

Democracy: systematically sounding out the opinions and aspirations of every person on the range of problems concerning their existence, and equally systematically searching for a peaceful and negotiated solution to the contradictions which thus emerge between different imperatives.

This book tries to move towards a realization of the first three values. Let us start, however, by looking at the fourth, at the *intimate* link between political ecology and the idea of democracy.

2

Ecology and Democracy

The Rio Conference in June 1992 suddenly brought environmental questions to centre stage in world diplomacy. Moreover, this United Nations Conference on Environment and
Development (UNCED) established close ties between the
environment and the whole range of human activities, and
therefore dealt with virtually everything which human beings
do on earth. There could no longer be any doubt at all that
ecology is essentially political.

Ecology as social relationships

The obvious reason for the interest in ecology, even at the
highest level, and for the fact that ecology is becoming explicitly political, is that there is a 'crisis of the environment'.
The bitterness, even the failure, of the preliminary negotiations at Rio clearly shows the real nature of 'the environment': it is what is done by other people, who make life
difficult for us, pollute us; by other nations, who go over the
top. *The environment is other people!* – just as we are, each
one of us, other people's environment. Ecology is a social
relationship, a relationship between human beings.

And what about nature? Ecology, it was thought, was about nature, and political ecology about the relationship between human beings and nature, a kind of unformulated opposite of the Marxists' 'productive forces'. Political ecology is certainly a social relationship, itself leading to a more specific relationship with what is *not* human activity, and which we call 'nature' or alternatively 'the environment', when the externality we are thinking about is too 'de-natured', for example, when it is clearly the result of social activity in the past – heritage, a local community, a shanty town, pastureland with trees, an artificial forest.

This externality of nature to human activity and this immersion of humanity in nature are essential. Marx, in his critique of socialism in its infancy, *Critique of the Gotha Programme*, starts by saying, 'It is not true to say that labour is the source of all wealth. Nature is just as much the source of use values (and it is surely of such values that wealth consists!) as labour, which itself is merely the expression of a natural force, the force of man's labour.' And in *Capital*, he went even further: 'Work is the father of wealth, but nature is its mother.' In other words, nature is the condition of any activity or wealth which is not itself the product of particular work; and ignorance of this 'mother' is the Achilles' heel of theoretical or applied socialism (as is its denial of the feminine – Marx's metaphor is gender-based!).[1] Being Green is first and foremost to be indignant that this precondition of our activity, this wealth which exists both for its own sake and for us, is itself disfigured and can be wiped out by irresponsible human behaviour.

This is the basic truth in 'deep ecology', as we are reminded by native peoples and the famous speech of Chief

Seattle, of the Dewamish tribe, in his reply to the American President who wanted to buy their land:

> We at least know this, that the Earth does not belong to humanity, humanity belongs to the Earth. This we know. Everything is interconnected, just as blood unites a family. Everything is interconnected, and everything that happens to the Earth happens to the children of the Earth. Humanity did not weave the tissue of life, it is merely a thread of it. Everything it does to this tissue, it does to itself.

However, we have to say that, just as humanity is part of nature, so nature is itself now humanized. Everything that exists on Earth is nowadays influenced by human activity – the stability of Himalayan mountain-sides, the porosity of soil, the acidity of water, the amount of carbon dioxide in the atmosphere, the biological diversity of the countryside, the thickness of the ozone layer. Humanity has become accountable for nature, the most powerful force on the planet.

It also has to be said that even 'natural nature' (the environment which is not yet a by-product of social activity – for example, the so-called 'virgin' forests) is a human asset to be preserved as such. Ecologists often make this assertion in the name of *beauty* – and they are right to do so. After discounting as necessary for the reproduction of societies almost all human activities (from war to eroticism, by way of production), there is nothing left as net product apart from the beautiful things handed down to future generations. In the debit column of the balance sheet are the beauties of nature borrowed from these future generations and handed back in a disfigured condition.

Here, even the best Marxist tradition (the early Marx, as seen in the *Economic and Philosophical Manuscripts of*

1844) is not enough for ecologists. When Marx calls on us to take account of nature because it is 'the inorganic body of humankind' (which humans would therefore have to absorb, appropriate – in a word, digest), he is imposing an anthropocentrism, which may well be legitimate for a scientist (conducting an ecology of a species is studying its 'external physiology', as people used to say).[2] However, this anthropocentrism can lead to the worst excesses, as in the demiurgical megalomaniac humanism of socialism in action in the Siberian taiga or the Kazakhstan steppes. Nature is not just the inorganic body of humankind. It is also the inorganic body of bees, bisons or golden eagles, and our organic bodies are also the inorganic body of worms . . . Stating these everyday truths is not being anti-humanist; it is the basis of the best kind of humanism, that of Pascal. Human beings are thinking reeds, the weakest beings in nature; but through thought they understand nature, that is, they are *responsible* for it, and they are the *only ones* in this position.

However, even when our governments claim not to know the 'existence value' of the beauty of nature (for example, of elephants, of snow-capped peaks or tropical forests), they are obliged to face the need to preserve this natural nature, as long as it is the condition of future activities. Wild species, and the biological diversity of these, are the 'immune system' of our biosphere, the ultimate safeguard against biological catastrophes. The atmosphere, in its 'preindustrial' state (that is, without the greenhouse gases from industry and agriculture which are gradually saturating it), was a condition of the emergence of our civilizations, and probably of their survival.

The already existing 'external framework' of all activities is the field of employment, and it is in respect of this central contested terrain that political ecology is a *relationship between each person and everybody else.*

A social relationship between each person and everybody else (and even every*thing* else)? At first sight, for the Marxist vulgate, this is an unusual social relationship. Marxists focused on 'contradictions', on relationships dividing and linking groups of human beings as social classes: masters and slaves, bourgeoisie and proletariat. Certainly these relationships are extremely important: they structure human activity, and determine the unequal distribution of wealth and freedom. Analysing (and denouncing) these relationships is a valued tradition of human consciousness. Marxists, however, are disorientated by this social relationship without a historical subject other than *each* and *everybody else*, the latter being in this context *all other users*, *all other polluters*, *all other peoples*, *all succeeding generations* and so on.

Nevertheless . . . humanity has learned to regulate, and the social sciences to identify, tensions of the 'between each and everybody' kind. It is the same relationship between the private producer and social production, regulated by the *market*, or between the citizen and the community, regulated by *politics*. The market and forms of politics (such as democracy) are therefore *already practical ecology*. It follows therefore that not only is ecology political, but politics and in particular democracy are already ecology!

The regulation of ecological contradictions

How is a 'contradiction' (as Marxists would say) – a relationship between each and everyone – to be regulated? In the same way as all social contradictions: by manners and customs (habits, values, or *habitus*, as the sociologist Pierre Bourdieu would say) and by institutions.

Regulating a relationship 'by manners and customs', 'through ideology' seems laughable in the present-day context. The time has long gone, it would seem, when Montesquieu argued that the principle behind democracy was virtue, when Marxists asserted that a 'new man' was needed to build socialism. 'Substantive democracy' (that is, the definition of democracy in terms of the *content*, of what it does for the community) is nowadays the object of derision, and democracy is reduced to the procedural ('how decisions are made').

Nevertheless, 'thou shalt not kill' was, and still is, the first significant principle of human ecology, and therefore of democracy. 'Social justice' (or at least a modicum of it!), as a norm for the state to have to respect, was the major achievement of the workers' movement. It is the task of ecology to extend 'thou shalt not kill' beyond social justice to international justice ('thou shalt not pollute others' habitats'), intergenerational justice ('thou art merely borrowing this planet from the next generation') and even justice between living species! In this sense, just as social democracy[3] transcended civil democracy, political ecology arguably transcends social democracy, in its *primarily moral* recognition of new rights, new entitlements and new objects of rights, giving rise to new duties and new interdicts. This could be the biggest step forward, and no mean achievement, of the Rio Conference and its hundreds of parallel conferences – the recognition, solemnly and in the full glare of publicity, of new rights and duties, to be incorporated as normal and on a par with honesty, respect for others and the Universal

Declaration of Human Rights. Rio laid the foundations of a 'case-law' justice in the absence of democratically established legislation.

This 'case-law' approach to the establishment of 'international ecological law', based on a universally recognized ecologist morality, will surprise quite a lot of continental Europeans, particularly those within the Marxist tradition. It will be much less of a surprise to activists and theorists in the English-speaking tradition. Many non-government environmentalist and development organizations complain not so much of a lack of law as of a weak judiciary – for them the problem lies in the *independence* of the judiciary which interprets the law.

A further point is that ecological manners and customs will flourish only in appropriate institutions. It is not just a matter of the majority of citizens being 'virtuous'; virtue must also have some encouragement from the law. Moreover, as we have seen, institutional forms for regulating contradictions between each and everybody already exist: they are either of the 'policy' kind or of the 'market' kind.

Ecological regulations of the *policy* kind are, in our culture, almost inevitably *statist*: standards, prohibitions, taxes and subsidies, and, above all, strategic choices about land-use planning and capital investment. In other words, in areas vital for the environment, what land should be designated, what infrastructure projects, what technical approach chosen? It goes without saying that it is essentially a matter of politics. The example of the French motorway programme and the difficulties of the Green government of the Nord–Pas-de-Calais region in challenging it, is a good illustration. The choice of a mode of transport is a state affair, a political matter. Representative democracy has a role which is of course crucial, but merely one role among several. What counts is adherence to this territorial authority on the part of the citizen. Information and public consultation are the first stage; the second stage is decision-making. Even more important is the next stage – acceptance by society of the political choice. It is no use replacing motorways by railways if car owners still use their cars.

Another example is that of choice of energy sources: should priority be given to nuclear energy (reducing the greenhouse effect)? Or to other energy sources, even polluting ones (reducing nuclear risk)? Or to energy saving (alleviating both risks at once)? It is a choice which involves, quite apart from technology, our lifestyle, a choice between different fears, a choice about sharing risks, a choice of responsibility. Political decision-making is therefore only a small link in an infinitely more complex chain of events in which a society imperils its own civilization. Political regulation is only a small part of ethical regulation. Less than ever, the role of elected political representatives is to have the last word. The political majority has to be persuaded and supported by a cultural majority.

What of the market? The market at least allows the decentralized expression of the 'price' which a civilization puts on the utility of the goods it produces or the measures it takes to protect the environment. Unfortunately this price reflects only the value of the good offered – the labour (the 'father' of wealth) required to produce it. The price does not reflect anything else. In particular it reflects the degradation of the 'great outside' (the 'mother') only if the law obliges it, through taxes, or through permits which can be bought and sold, in other words, by 'internalizing external costs'.[4] Politics, in the shape of democracy, is therefore already there in the foundations of an 'ecological market economy'.

Regulating access to nature through the market involves firstly an initial share-out of rights to this access, then establishing instruments to regulate access, and finally institutionalizing the location and mechanisms of exchange. All this is eminently political. Nevertheless, in a world where pollution is everywhere and is felt everywhere, it is probably the only way of decentralized regulation. This is why Anil Agarwal's proposal to regulate 'greenhouse' gases is so important; the proposal was supported by non-governmental organizations in the environment and development fields at the Ya Wananchi World Conference in Paris in December 1991. The proposal was to establish quotas, country by country, transferable between countries (on a chargeable basis), of the right to emit greenhouse gases. Taxes on these emissions would have similar effects, and there would be a mix of both quotas and taxes. There are two problems however. First, the market economy does not exist everywhere (one cannot use taxes against nomadic slash-and-burn farmers); more importantly, the initial allocation of rights to use nature remains a purely political question.

After all, it boils down to a question of ending free access to those 'common goods of humanity' such as the atmosphere or biological diversity – the subjects of two major agreements negotiated and signed at Rio; it involves ending free access to nature. Humanity has to look itself in the face every time it emits carbon gas or isolates a gene. The whole international debate on these major issues will perhaps one day lead to market regulation, but this will have been *instituted* by political agreement – an international political agreement more or less respecting the equality of humans with regard to life. In other words, a more or less democratic agreement. In real terms, will rights over the atmosphere be allocated to countries according to population, or according to their present level of pollution?

Here, interstate regulation through diplomacy clearly takes on a political dimension, in the sense in which Marxists would recognize the term. In fact, what will happen is not very different from the great founding event of capitalism – the enclosure of common land at the end of the Middle Ages. This was a time when 'free pasture' on common land could not ensure the ecological balance of the European country-side, threatened by demographic pressure, feudal pressure, the ravages of war and so on. Poverty was endemic, the Black Death came and destroyed everything. The common lands had to be allocated to people who had the skills and re-sources to exploit them; they were given to 'rich ploughmen', and the rest were proletarianized. I share the fear of Anil Agarwal that regulating the protection of the atmosphere – a necessary measure which has provoked an alliance of old and new fanatics of pollution, the United States and Malaysia – will become an enormous expropriation of the right of poor countries to breathe.[5]

A participatory ecological democracy

The state (or a concert of states) is therefore a stage of ecological regulation which is necessary, but limited and even dangerous. It is limited because it represents the general interest only in the form of an 'externality', a power above us, whereas the need is to internalize, in his or her behaviour, each individual's duty to everyone. It is dangerous because (as traditional Marxists knew full well!), since the state is 'external', separate from the community, it can be appropriated by a minority. As for the market, that is even worse, since it is directly controlled by those who have long had most wealth; and, unless the state again intervenes to redistribute it, there is no hope of a reversal of this situation.

Do we escape from ecological risk only by further increasing the power of these two leviathans? Not necessarily, since politics is not just about the state. It is the organized confrontation of interests; in its origins, it is the social construction of the representation of identities and interests. The market, diplomacy and even representative democracy arrive on the scene 'after the event', when interests are already well entrenched. Interests, customs and manners, and implied compromises are established beforehand, or outside the framework of political struggle and competition, through debate and face-to-face encounters. These themselves should be organized, and in particular by the famous non-governmental organizations (NGOs) which showed how important they were on the fringe of the Rio Conference.

An unfortunate example, first of all: the huge urban sprawl of São Paulo, where two thirds of housing is 'informal' (that is, not regulated by the state), obtains its water from reservoirs separated by a zone where no building is allowed. However, already a million *favellados* (shanty-town dwellers) have infiltrated this zone. Illegal construction of *favellas*, often by 'radical' activists of the Workers' Party, goes on in the name of a 'right to housing' as opposed to 'bourgeois legality'; but it is getting perilously close to the reservoirs. In the face of this threat, compounded by the fear of cholera,

the São Paulo municipal authorities, controlled by the Workers' Party, were ready to send in the military. This is a tragic
example of this social relationship (ecology) which does not
set one class against another but 'everyone against each'.
Poor people, for the sake of the right to housing, are depriv-
ing other poor people of the right to drinking water! It is not
enough to say that socialist reform of the grossly unequal
Brazilian society would mean a solution of the housing problem; in any event, this would take time. A contradiction such
as this can only be settled peacefully by face-to-face democracy, by mutual understanding of everybody's interests. It is
necessary, of course, for these interests to be expressed, and
therefore organized.

The only way to fight effectively for *sustainable development*, that is, for the rights of nature and future generations,
while respecting the right of present generations to establish
the material conditions of their welfare, and the only way to
reconcile 'environment' and 'development' (to oversimplify
a much more complex debate), is if these rights are *organized*
to allow the most direct possible confrontation between
them. The best way would be for this confrontation to replace direct political regulation – in any event this is the ideal
we should strive for. This was the near-unanimous conclusion from meetings organized by NGOs in Paris, Rio and
elsewhere, around the Earth Summit. In other words, tropical forests would be better protected by the confrontation of
the short- and long-term interests of those who live from
them, than by intervention by some High Authority of a
Security Council type, armed with green helmets.

One of the most significant steps forward arising from
debates around the Rio Conference was in fact this push by
NGOs from all over the world, whether environment- or

development-based, for a solution through participatory democracy. It was at Rio that we again discovered that, since ecology has become political, it is up to politics – and its most elevated form, democracy – to become what it always was: ecological.

3

Political Ecology and the Workers' Movement: Similarities and Differences

My aim in this chapter is not to deal with the link between ecology and socialism as politico-social movements. I outlined in the Preface how my thinking on this had developed: from *environment* as a kind of Second Front of the workers' movement, to a rainbow-like juxtaposition of social movements equal by right, and finally to the supremacy of the *green paradigm* in that it encompasses the emancipatory aspirations of the workers' movement and extends them to the whole of the relationships between human beings and between them and nature.

Since this move from Red to Green is fairly common not only in France, and since this book is mainly for those who, like me, became Green after being Red (or Pink), I want in this chapter to look at the common features and differences between what was 'Red' and what is now, for many of us, 'Green'. Readers who do not feel at home with these intellectual 'itineraries' and shifts should skip this chapter!

By 'Red' and 'Green', I mean social movements as well as the ideology or world view which gives them some kind of cohesion. Already we have a profound similarity: in both cases, a unity is claimed between a social movement (workers' movement, ecologist movement) and a theory (Marxism, scientific ecology). In both cases, moreover, this unity is not total. The workers' movement cannot be defined in terms of those factions whose point of reference is a particular social theory, whether Marxist or not. Mutualism and much of syndicalism have no theoretical reference. The same applies to conservationist movements, naturalist movements (though the latter are based on the natural sciences) or more generally environmentalist movements. What I am looking at here, therefore, are movements of *political* ecology where, in Europe as in North and South America, many recruits are people who have had enough of 'scientific socialism'.

A similarity which is almost continuity

Similarities between Red and Green are all the more noticeable in that, in many cases, political ecology imported methods and inspiration from 'the Red'. This continuity was such that, with the 'Grünen' of northern Germany for example, there was sometimes a convergence in reverse with the former East German Communist Party. The continuity, however, does not come about only by 'infiltration'. The main reason why many Reds are now Green is that they *left* the Red, and broke with socialism, even, as we will see later, in its ideal form; a secondary reason is that when political ecology movements first appeared, they saw a kind of 'family likeness' to what they were in before – we can list these as materialism, dialectics, historicism and a progressive orientation.

Materialism

Political ecology, like the socialist workers' movement, is based on a critique, and therefore an analysis or theorized knowledge, of 'the existing order of things'. From that any utopia can flourish or any realism founder. However, people who are Red or Green have one other thing in common – a taste for knowledge of 'what is happening'. By inclination, they are encyclopaedists, as eighteenth-century liberals were.

More particularly, Reds and Greens focus on a very specific sector of reality: the relationship between humanity and nature, and even more precisely, relationships between people in so far as they concern nature – what Marxists called 'productive forces'. Of course, Reds and Greens are totally opposed in the way they interpret this relationship, seen as positive by the former but negative by the latter. The former acclaim the appropriation of nature by humans, the latter denounce this spoliation, and, when it comes to 'deep ecology', acclaim nature's capacity of self-regulation when predatory humans are not present. In any event, ecologists see indigenous peoples, rightly or wrongly, as having an innate capacity for natural symbiosis – a 'primitive sustainable development', as it were – just as 'scientific socialists' acclaimed primitive communism.

I will look again at this fundamental difference, but for the moment let us simply note the similarity of mental pathologies deriving from this common materialism:

1 The tendency to scientism, ignoring the legitimacy of conflicts of interest between people, and ignoring the political implications.
2 The assertion of a 'correct' relationship between humans and nature: 'orthodox' Marxists extol the *progress of science and industry*, ecologists acclaim *natural equilibria*.
3 The utopia of a return to cybernetics, a regulation of the humanity–nature relationship, shorn of its social, democratic and conflictual aspect: 'moving from government of people to administration of things' for Marxists; 'living in harmony with nature' for proponents of 'deep ecology'.

It is also amusing to observe how James Lovelock's[1] 'cult of Gaia', of Earth as a living being, a mystical departure from the scientific hypothesis of the same name (itself already full of ambiguities), fulfils exactly the same function as the Stalinist cult of progress, both among ecologists with the greatest need to boost their commitment by belief (the New Age tendency), and among enemies of political ecology. Even though the cult of Gaia is virtually unknown in France, Luc Ferry[2] is an example of somebody who denounces ecology as being the subordination of any individual will to the demands of Moloch-Gaia, just as in the past socialism was equated with Stalinism! The argument becomes particularly grotesque when it emanates from proponents of the old 'progressivism' – the progressivism of the 'forces of science and industry', as in the Heidelberg appeal.[3]

Dialectics

The materialism of the Greens, like that of the 'Reds', is in fact much more a *critique* of the existing disorder than an exaltation of an underlying order or the predication of a new order. Marxists based their approach on a critique of political economy as it actually existed in order to guarantee its overthrow; in the same way, ecologists denounce ecology as it actually exists (relationship between humanity and its environment) in order to stress its non-sustainability. In fact, both recount history in the same way – there is a critique of real structures by social movements which are real, and which are brought into existence by the very structures they are against.

Even more profoundly, Greens and Reds are at one in their emphasis on two themes:

1 The theme of *totality*: just as the theory of the workers' movement was not merely 'social economy', but a global vision of social relationships (political, ideological . . .), similarly the object of political economy is not the 'environment' but the totality – humanity *and* its environment *and* human activity supported by the environment and transforming it . . .

2 The theme of *interrelationships*: this totality is perceived as a system, with relatively autonomous levels and elements, but where everything has an effect on everything else.

We see in these two approaches all the conceptual paraphernalia of dialectics or cybernetics, in particular positive retroactive loops (the snowball effect) and negative retroactions (the dampening or regulating effect). And of course there will be the political counterparts of these: catastrophism and meliorism.

The tendencies insisting on the 'snowball development' hold that pre-existing limitations (in humanity, in nature and so on) will bring about an abrupt catastrophic halt. On this basis, it is laughable, even futile and suspect, to try to stop an avalanche: it is better to wait for the inevitable catastrophe, then build a better world once the past has been swept away. Those, on the other hand, who opt for self-regulating mechanisms where reality creates its own antidotes, will regard their own actions as an antidote to 'the free play of market forces', or the frenzied appetites of capitalism or productivism. It will even be possible to take account of the need for self-limitation of one's demands, so as not to run the risk of provoking, in reaction to imbalances, demands which are even more serious. The crisis will be forgotten, as will the *drift to extremes* dear to Lenin; and the politics of the possible will prevail . . . with history, or Gaia, going its own sweet way.

Historicism

After all, Greens share with Reds the conviction that they are coming on the scene at a time when the owl of Minerva is flying away, when a particular form of the order of things is taking us so close to catastrophe that the Big Change is due: the Revolution, the altered paradigm, the change of era . . .

This Great Form which has to be swept away is called 'capitalism' by the workers' movement, and 'productivism' by political ecology. By 'productivism', Greens mean the whole set of socio-economic structures and mentalities which push people to 'produce for the sake of producing', with no care for the real needs of people or the sustainability of the production regime (that is, the possibility of applying this regime over time without jeopardizing the conditions for satisfying the needs of future generations, and particularly the survival of ecosystems). As is clear, Greens do not address a priori the burning question posed by historians: is it

mentalities which determine the consolidation of social structures, or vice versa? All of which means that it is no surprise
to them that pre-existing mentalities survive revolutions.
This difference is therefore far from neutral, but it is clear
that productivism for Greens is exactly what capitalism is for
Reds – what needs to be got rid of in order to change the
world. In fact, it was convenient to speak of productivism
when it was a matter of denouncing capitalism and the model
of so-called 'socialist' countries in the same breath. Now a
days, when 'socialism in action' is nothing more than a bad
memory, Greens will tend more and more to admit that
productivism and capitalism are the same thing.

Productivism or capitalism: either way, it is a case of
stretching to breaking point the tensions in relationships between human beings, and between them and nature. A
threshold has been crossed, and today the political ecology
movement has come into being, just as in the past the
workers' movement was born. With these movements lies
the historical (or millenarian?) responsibility for mounting
the final great battle: 'socialism or barbarism' in the past,
'ecology or death' today.

Corresponding to this similar development is once again a
common pathology: catastrophism, the arrogance of the
prophet, disregard for the lessons of the past, all the surprises
of a history which, as Lenin said, 'has infinitely more
imagination than we have'.

Political progressivism

As already mentioned in passing – and it will crop up again –
ecology diverges from the workers' movement on the crucial

point of the 'progress of productive forces'. However, though Greens no longer believe in a transhistorical material movement which would guarantee human progress, they are quite willing to be placed in the tradition of all humanity's emancipation movements, both before and after the workers' movement: universalism, democracy, socialism (in its libertarian guise), Third Worldism, feminism, regionalism . . . They are therefore at one with Reds in all their historical struggles, and denounce parties claiming to be socialist when these abandon their own social objectives, such as reduction in working time, civil rights for resident foreigners and so on.

Seeing eye to eye like this in no way stems from an opportunistic extension of the area of political preoccupations beyond the 'initial core' of environmentalism. It is perfectly possible to move from environmentalism to political ecology and *therefore* to the fight for reduced working time and the new citizenship; but a necessary stage is still adherence to the 'historical and dialectical materialism' peculiar to Greens, and referred to above.

In a nutshell: Greens are political progressives because they are opposed to productivism. This means that they are of necessity on the side of the dominated against the dominators; on the side of the workers (wage-earners or peasants) when they revolt against the reduction of their activity to an entrance ticket into the consumer society; on the side of the Third World against the imperialist pillage of their land, peoples and cultures. Against the social and international relations of productivism, they set a project of a new model of development, 'sustainable development', or 'ecodevelopment', just as Reds set socialism against capitalism.

This political progressivism of Greens naturally exposes them to the same shortcomings as Reds – an example is the tendency to divide the world into 'good and bad', 'us and them'. This tendency is easily combined with scientism, as in the case of scientific socialism: *we are the ones who know* against *those who pretend not to know what they are doing.* Another example is the tendency to utopianism, the ideology of the New Jerusalem: 'Here, with productivism, we can do nothing, because it dominates everything. But when we leave this valley of tears, when we can build a new world, just you see!'

All in all, Green shows very strong resemblances to Red. Both are 'principles of hope'[4] with similar origins: materialist (the starting point is a critical knowledge of the real world), dialectical (the expectation is that the real world will give rise to its own material critique), historical ('the time has come!') and progressive. On this score, Green also shares most of the risks of Red, and reveals its flaws: there have been frequent denunciations of the 'fundamentalism' of German or French Greens (as an exact analogy of 'Leftism'); it is likely we will soon see condemnation of their 'realism' (analogous to the old 'opportunism').

Reformulations

Green has nevertheless one significant advantage over Red: it postdates it, by more than a century of trial and error. The Green paradigm developed on its own basis, but this included a theoretical and practical critique of the Red paradigm. A principle of hope was developing in a way which was similar, but not the same – a reformulation of the principle of hope.

The basic difference between the two has already been examined: the idea of a 'progress through productive forces' entailing other kinds of progress is completely absent from the Green paradigm. At worst, political ecology mistrusts any growth of productive forces (that is, domination of humanity over nature), and at best it asserts that a different relationship between human beings would mean a better relationship between humans and nature. Like Althusserian or Maoist versions of Marxism, political ecology rejects the primacy of productive forces; it subordinates them to social relationships and to the vision of the world which inspires these. It judges human–nature relationships not on the basis of *control*, but on the basis of *respect* – of human beings, of future generations and even of other species.

The first consequence is immediate: political ecology has a rather negative opinion of many of the 'successes' of socialism, in its Stalinist version obviously (where socialism in action was one of the most barbaric kinds of productivism), but also in its social democratic version (unrestricted growth of mass consumption). This conflict about end results – and even about objectives – between ecologists on the one hand and socialists and communists on the other is well known, and there is no need to go into further details here.

The second consequence is more far-reaching: the Green paradigm is certainly politically progressive, but it is not a 'progressivism', since its vision of history is not the history of a progression. In fact, it is not in any way a vision of history directed to anything. One cannot use the paradigm to write history 'in the future perfect' (as in 'this harrowing past will have prepared for a shining future'). If history were directed towards something, this would be by the second principle of thermodynamics – the history of an inexorable growth of entropy, the history of a degradation. Only self-critical human consciousness can slow down or reverse this degradation. Political ecology can define progress only as *direction*, defined in terms of a certain number of ethical or aesthetic values (solidarity, autonomy, responsibility, democracy, harmony . . .); all this without any material guarantee that the world will in fact go in this direction (through the 'socialization of productive forces'). The historical and dialectical materialism of Greens is 'non-teleological' (that is, it is not directed towards an ultimate end), and it is even rather pessimistic.

This move away from the primacy of productive forces has another consequence: a move away from the primacy of producers. The reason why the Greens, as politically progressive, are often on the side of the exploited and the oppressed is that their values, the ecology of the world they dream of, are against exploitation and oppression. It is in no way because they would regard producers exploited by productivism as themselves the vehicles of the consciousness of a world without productivism (some people at this point might say, 'On the contrary . . .'). The disorder of the world engenders social movements of critical resistance, but none has primacy over others, except in its own field. The *autonomous* expression of the interests and aspirations of social movements independent of each other is the precondition of their possible future convergence in a Green paradigm, but this convergence would only be a political and social construction.

To say 'political construction' (of the unity of social forces) is to run the risk of thinking in terms of 'construction through politics' (of this unity); that is to say, by means of the state and, in the meantime, through the party. After all, this was

how the problem was solved by those in the workers' movement who had doubts about the consciousness, within the
working class, of its historical mission (as did Lenin in *What
is to be Done?*). This is the trap awaiting ecologist parties –
since there is no social movement carrying *the* ecologist consciousness, it would be up to the party to decide what, at any
given time, is ecologist and what is merely 'nimbyist' (the
Green equivalent of trade unionism, of straightforward
syndical consciousness in the workers' movement). For
example, should we, for the sake of the fight against the
greenhouse effect from motor cars, build a high-speed
railway line in the Rhône Valley, when this would mean
destroying a valley and its hillsides? Should we, for the sake
of the right to be different, allow students to wear Islamic
headscarves in schools? And so on.

A good point is that Green is lucky to have come after
Red, on the basis of a libertarian critique of the 'party leadership' and the demiurgical role of the state. The principle
of autonomy of social movements is not a corrective or a
counterweight, but a *component value* of the Green paradigm. Face-to-face, participatory democracy, the search for a
consensus of divergent viewpoints, the right to a dissensus,[5]
are rooted in a culture of rejection of regulations dictated
from on high. Obviously, it is not a guarantee: the same
causes (fragmentation of popular aspirations, the complex
nature of reality) will tend to produce the same effects
(externalization of political mediation; tendency to say, 'the
ecologist party is better than associations, because it has a
higher perspective of things'). But the experience may serve
to stop us from going over the same ground again.

This is all the more so in that consciousness of the complexity of the real world, and of the large number of contra-

dictions, absence of any idea of 'last-resort determination' by a particular social relationship (the economy, the consumption of energy, or some other), absence of a social movement regarded as 'central', all leads as far as Greens are concerned to the non-availability of a determining moment in the historical process (such as the Reds have) – assuming supreme power. When Greens are asked whether they are reformists or revolutionaries, even the most 'fundamentalist' among them are at a loss for a reply, quite simply because they cannot see what would be *the* point of application of an 'ecologist political revolution'. They are in favour of changing many things, but power as such, state power, is hardly in their sights. It would change neither work relations, nor consumer mentalities, nor relations between the sexes. As heirs of Michel Foucault and Félix Guattari rather than Marxism, they dream of a multitude of small breaks with the past, of a molecular revolution never completed. They know that being in power can get things done, help struggles along, influence relationships based on relative strengths, but also that the main thing is happening elsewhere – in changes to myriad behaviour patterns.

Political ecology is therefore in danger of making many mistakes. It is relatively safe from the danger of totally sinking into one huge monstrous error. This one fact makes it, more than the workers' movement, profoundly materialist: a movement of the real world, in the real world, for the real world.

Paraphrasing a declaration of faith which is often ignored, one could say that Greens do not have interests different from other citizens concerned about the harmony of relationships between humans and with nature. In every partial ecologist struggle, they are simply trying to assert the viewpoint of the movement as a whole and to be the most determined. They ought not to try to dictate arrogantly to others what a correct policy would be, but rather to convince others, by the correctness of their proposals and the example of what they do, to unite in a common struggle in favour of life.

4

The Rise and Fall of Economic Liberalism

The major enemy of political ecology as the twentieth century comes to a close – the biggest threat to the planet, blocking sustainable development, provoking global social tensions and splitting society into haves and have-nots – is not any kind of productivism, or even capitalism, but the model of capitalist development which, throughout the 1980s, claimed to offer a way out of the crisis through a return to economic liberalism.

In fact, the 1980s seemed at first sight to mark the triumph of economic liberalism, with the longest period of American growth, the collapse of the rotten edifice of 'socialism', the end of 'new approaches' in the Third World, the disappearance of Marxism and greater selfishness and individualism. However, 1990 saw a change of fortune, with recession in Britain and the United States, and despite the dollar falling to less than half its 1985 yen or Deutschmark value, an enormous trade deficit which stretched to 10 billion dollars a month in a seven-year period at the end of the 1980s and the beginning of the 1990s. Hard-pressed, the United States alone had a debt of more than half that of the whole of the Third World. One by one, its firms fell into the hands of better 'organized', less liberal, countries such as Germany and Japan. To make ends meet, the American government was forced to hire out its huge army – the price tag of the Gulf War was 51 billion dollars (half a year's trade deficit), picked up by the Arab emirs, Germany and Japan. The Third World saw the downturn of countries like Argentina and Peru, with their declared (or IMF-imposed) neo-liberalism, and the triumph of protectionist, quasi-planned economy countries such as South Korea and Taiwan. At the December 1990 Geneva GATT talks, American attempts to impose free trade in services and agriculture foundered on European, Japanese and Korean resistance. Two years later, the talks were about how to organize the share-out of market volumes, and the new American President, Bill Clinton, rejected even more firmly the economic liberalism which had ruined his country.

The end of Fordism

Twenty years previously, the developed world had seen the triumph of a model of capitalist development often called 'Fordism', combining an *organization of work* ('Taylorism') which set the originators of ideas against the supposedly passive and disciplined 'operatives', and a tripartite agreement between employers, unions and state to 'redistribute the fruits of growth' in the domestic market. This model, not of course a very 'liberal' one, was thrown into crisis when the organization of work became less and less efficient, and the tripartite agreement was made impracticable by the internationalization of production and markets.

The ideological and political victory of Thatcherism in the United Kingdom (1979) and Reaganism in the United States

(1981) was not only a turning point in the global sense, as seen in the 1980 Venice Summit and Mitterrand's rather unexpected conversion in 1983, but also a change within those countries to economic liberalism, which gave the go-ahead to 'production for production's sake' – liberal productivism. The acceptance of this by public opinion was mainly due to the crisis of previous compromises; and as a response, it had many weaknesses.[1]

First, it in no way solved the crisis of the organization of work, but simply endorsed it by concluding that employees should be treated less generously than they were under Fordism. It merely fell in with the anarchy of international competition by saying that each country should export as much as possible, and by implication have the lowest possible wage costs and the flimsiest possible social (and environmental) legislation.

The consequences of liberal productivism were abundantly clear – former Fordist countries choosing this path were Third Worldized, 'Brazilianized', with social polarization, urban ghettos, the reappearance of 'social evils' such as drugs and Aids, and of racism and so on. Street disturbances involving looting, well known in the Third World, spread to the United States, the United Kingdom and, at the end of the 1980s, to France, at Mantes-la-Jolie and Vaulx-en-Velin. The United States, the fifteenth country in the world on the United Nations index of human development (a combination of per capita income, life expectancy and educational achievement), has the best-paid employers in the world, just ahead of Brazil and Argentina, whereas average wages dropped to their 1962 levels.

However, another, totally opposite, approach became possible: a different kind of compromise between capital and labour, with a 'mobilization of human resources' in the implementation of new technologies in return for more far-reaching social guarantees, increased living standards and even, in Germany, reduction in working time. This approach was adopted by most exporters in Japan, Germany, Scandinavia and the 'Alpine arc' of Switzerland, Austria and northern Italy. Obviously, this new solution to the 'supply-side crisis' did not solve the question of turmoil in world markets, but against all expectation it was more competitive in those markets, and the highest-paid and best socially 'guaranteed' workers (Germans and Japanese) ensured that their employers easily won out over their American, British and French competitors.

Triumphs and disasters of economic liberalism in the East and the South

This remarkable defeat of economic liberalism was largely ignored in less developed countries – the former socialist countries and the rest of the Third World.

'Socialism' was simply a kind of state capitalism with a management–worker compromise rather different from Fordism. Here, Taylorism never worked properly, because management was incompetent and planning impossible; yet the wage relation was nevertheless more inflexible than in the case of Fordism (a situation which could be described as 'wage tenure'), though the price of this was fairly low wage levels. 'Socialism' as another possible compromise ('They pretend to pay us, so we pretend to work', as Polish workers used to say) was protected from Western competition by state monopoly of foreign trade. While 'socialism' collapsed, people did not choose an alternative model. The aim could have been a smooth transition to classic social democracy (Taylorism plus social rights), but most leaders in the East eagerly embraced the Thatcher–Reagan model of free trade and greater flexibility of labour. The result was the total collapse of all that had been achieved previously; and the single remaining hope for the elites is to replace the Third World as suppliers of ultra-flexible cheap labour. However, they are forgetting one thing: even in the 1990s, thousands of millions of people in countries from Morocco to East Asia have a standard of living much lower than in Poland or Russia; of these people, there are hundreds of millions who can produce and export more efficiently than Eastern Europe.

The same revolution took place in the 1970s and 1980s in the South. Here the first industrialization policy was in the period after the 1940s, when the United Nations Economic Commission for Latin America,[2] together with 'Third-Worldist' Western intellectuals, called for import substitution. This was a kind of combination of sub-Fordism and 'socialism' – tariff barriers, heavy state involvement in the economy to make up for the lack of an entrepreneurial class, and a compromise with a 'workers' aristocracy' propping up populist regimes.

Towards the end of the 1960s, this model suffered from the dual crisis of Fordism and 'socialism'. Neo-liberalism used attacks by free-market theorists (the 'Chicago boys') on Chile and Argentina as its training ground; by the 1990s its political victory throughout Latin America was complete. In Bolivia, for example, all existing compromises were ended with the slogan 'Hyperinflation = wage indexing = trade unionism'.

However, the economic consequences of this victory are themselves catastrophic – these 'newly de-industrialized countries' are in recession. Only Chile, paradoxically and despite mammoth debt, seems to have found a new equilibrium, by going back to its 'old' commodity-exporting specialization – copper, to which it has added citrus fruits and grapes. What remained of the working class produced by forty years of import substitution lives in the 1990s on odd jobs in shanty towns. However, the democratic coalition which replaced Pinochet hardly dared jeopardize this shabby achievement, quoting the debt constraint to justify the new-but-not-new export model. Argentina, and even Brazil, were bent on emulating Chile in a wave of destruction from which, by the mid-1990s, nothing positive had emerged.

In the Far East, however, the picture is quite different. Export-led industrialization was from the beginning based on extremely low wages (for women in particular), but also on far-reaching and well-protected agrarian reform (in Korea and Taiwan), and above all on the efficient planning of loans and capital equipment imports. These have been the 'winning countries' in terms of the South, and they threaten the Reaganist or Thatcherite North, which in the 1990s has to protect itself by tariff barriers. Korea and Taiwan have already begun to apply 'post-Taylorian' methods and to distribute the dividends to their working classes.

Neither in the North nor in the South has economic liberalism been victorious; but its success has been enough to ruin whole countries, in the North as well as the South, and to unbalance the world economy for many years to come.

Some countries responded by showing that they would be better off in intercapitalist competition with a form of capitalism which was more organized, more concerted, negotiating (in return for 'social advantages') the involvement of its workers in the fight for quality and productivity, and often at the forefront in matters of environmental protection. Even these countries, however, are powerless against world economic disorder: Sweden and Japan, the two highest-ranking countries according to the UN's index of human development, were not immune from the 1991–3 recession. Germany was unable to cope with the effects of a reunification which could have been better managed, as the German Greens made clear in 1989.[3] Finally, although these countries proved that economic liberalism *could* be improved on, at both the social and the environmental level, in no way can they (especially not Japan) serve as a model of 'sustainable development'.

The way forward, as far as the economy of a country such as France is concerned, is discussed in the next chapter; part II covers the international aspects of the crisis.

5

Ecology as Post-Socialist Economic Logic

From socialism to ecology

The final combat for Marx was against the first socialist movement to be institutionalized on a permanent basis. This was the German Social Democratic Party, the archetype of all parties of the Second and Third, and even the Fourth, Internationals. Marx's *Critique of the Gotha Programme*, as already mentioned on page 9, denied that labour is the source of all wealth.[1]

It is highly likely that, in Marx's mind, this critique did not go far enough. For him, nature was simply another factor of production, to be transcended socially and to be 'humanized' (see his *Economic and Philosophical Manuscripts of 1844*), in any event to be used, in the great Judaeo-Christian–Cartesian tradition. Moreover, for him nature was only a 'source' (of raw materials, of energy), as it later was in the first major 'anti-productivist' manifesto of the 1970s, the *Report of the Club of Rome*. Nowadays, ecologists are much less afraid about resource exhaustion, and have lighted on the basic problem: the limits of nature as a 'sink' (for waste and by-products), or as a place where people quite simply do things. In any event, Marx put his finger on one of the two basic 'blind spots' of socialism: the existence of a freely available 'environment', costing people nothing though available to be appropriated (hence Marx's interest in property rents), an expansion area which work cannot reconstitute, but which is necessary to capitalist accumulation.

The whole of socialism, in its social democratic or Stalinist versions, depended on ignorance about this. The compromise between capital (including capital in the guise of the state) and labour rested on the denial of this point.[2] The second major 'blind spot' was the denial of the oppression of women. Political ecology started as a rejection not only of economic liberalism, which, though longer established, was clearly based on the same premise, but also of this kind of socialism. At the same time, feminism, often allied to political ecology (or rather, a component of political ecology), rejected the second denial.

However, the core of political ecology is not 'the environment', but a complex totality consisting of a triangle: humankind, its activity and nature, nature under threat and transformed by human activity, nature which is both the matrix and the basis of this activity. In this sense, pasture with hedgerows, forestry plantations, urban areas, even shanty towns are, despite their artificiality, 'the environment'. The sources of ecological commitment may be love of humankind, love of nature, or a liking for harmony, but the *target* of political ecology can only be this decisive mediation between humankind and its environment – humanity's activity in producing, transforming and consuming. In other words, the economy. Economy and ecology – almost the same word. The former stresses 'calculation' (*nomos*),

the latter 'meaning' (*logos*). Ecologist economics is therefore
an activity which is calculated, and guided, by a certain
meaning.[3]

For ecologists, three basic values must guide human activity. Clearly, the first is *responsibility* – towards nature, i.e.
other species, and towards future generations from whom we
borrow this world, and to whom we will return it, transformed for better or for worse. This value is, as it were,
ecology's 'patent', its contribution to the long history of the
progress of human consciousness. However, political ecology
(in France as elsewhere) looks to other, longer-established
values inherited from earlier emancipation movements such
as political liberalism and socialism. Of these values, it
emphasizes two in particular – *autonomy* and *solidarity*.
Autonomy, the desire to be in control of one's activity, to see
one's actions through, asserted itself in the period after May
1968. It was sustained by the libertarian heritage in the face
of an economy which was too centralized and too technocratic – how could one feel a sense of responsibility when
excluded from economic decision-making processes? However, when many people who had experienced 1968 drifted
into individualism, ecologists clung to the imperative of *solidarity* – how could one care about future generations and
at the same time ignore those who were excluded and
marginalized at the present time?

These aims and imperatives are the link between the
new social movements which since the early 1970s have
been challenging the established disorder; they also inspire
and influence current developments in the trade unions
and even in the more enlightened sectors of the business
world.

A different way of working

Ecologist economics is first and foremost a different way of working, with emphasis placed on forms of activity undertaken by small groups in urban or rural areas, community groups, or co-operatives. Above all, however, the emphasis is on transformation of the wage relation itself – the 'negotiated mobilization of human resources', i.e. the intelligence, experience and imagination of working people, striving for quality products and a secure and efficient productive organization.[4] Not 'individualized merit payments', but on the contrary the organized (sometimes conflictual) co-operation of work communities.

This *negotiated involvement* of producers is the basis for everything. Redefinition of the true meaning of work and rediscovery of a chunk of autonomy at workshop or office level will be the basis of an extended citizenship, not only at work but in all aspects of social life and, of course, of ecological responsibility. Only producers aware of how they produce and concerned with how their work is organized will be able to impose the right production processes, for themselves and also for what is around them, for their customers and their product users. As we saw in the previous chapter, in the 1980s this new way of organizing work proved itself just as competitive as Taylorism. However, it does not automatically involve solidarity – the example of big Japanese companies, or top-performance industries in Baden-Württemberg, shows how risky it is to establish a 'wage-earning aristocracy' jealous of its own powers and privileges, hostile to solidarity with workers in other industries or less well-off regions. How far negotiation extends outside the firm (to the whole of the sector, or society in general) will be decisive, and therefore so will the state of mind of trade unionism.

Ecologist economics is also about the choice (again negotiated by a community enlightened as to its responsibilities) of the products of this activity. Too often, concern for 'the environment' is presented as a cost added to the price of products and possibly threatening jobs. However, *the opposite is true: the environment costs nothing*, and this is why it is squandered by productivism. Pollution and degradation of the biosphere are the costs which need to be eliminated! Today, these costs are met by nobody, or rather they are met by everybody. Meeting these costs does not mean imposing new costs, but simply making them visible and getting the polluters to pay them. In any event, future generations would have to pay them, and those now suffering from pollution are already paying them.

Concern for the environment, restoring and improving this heritage for future generations, can even become one of the main thrusts of economic activity, instead of the overconsumption of the first three post-war decades. In other words, instead of setting aside agricultural land in Europe to satisfy United States demands, instead of limiting 'competitive' agriculture to fewer and fewer hectares saturated with more and more pesticides and fertilizers, a reasoned reform of the Common Agricultural Policy should aim for the most biological agriculture possible, using lots of land and few chemical additives, but intensive in skilled farm labour, producing healthy and tasty food mainly for the domestic market, and keeping the countryside harmonious and varied. Similarly, it is often more economical to go for energy saving rather than extra productive capacity – dangerous in the case of nuclear energy, polluting in the case of coal and oil power stations, and land-greedy in the case of hydro-electricity. Moreover, in all cases energy saving creates, at constant expenditure levels, more jobs than producing more energy by power station and huge dam mega-schemes.

The final point is that ecologist economics involves a new form of distribution to match the progress of the 'happiness which comes from living'. In countries where the needs of a majority are guaranteed, it is absolutely essential that the distribution of productivity gains should have two guiding principles: the *fight against social exclusion* and *non-material growth*, i.e. of free time. This is why the reduction of working time is at the core of ecologist macroeconomics.

The revolution of free time

In the form of 'work sharing', new thinking about free time is above all a prime expression of *solidarity*. All that the French Left government of the 1980s managed to do, in its pursuit of Keynesian or free-market models, was to push unemployment up to 3 million, with the accompanying misfortunes of social exclusion, ghettos, crime and racism. Putting back together a society which has been torn apart is today's prime imperative, too long hidden by expectation of a mythical economic recovery. This recovery duly happened in the second half of the 1980s, but it hardly dented the unemployment figures, and the subsequent recession further inflated them. It is therefore the height of cynicism to claim that 'only growth will reduce unemployment'. In fact, the only way to stop unemployment growing is to reduce the *individual*'s working time, continuing the long-standing trend halted in the early 1980s. My proposal is an immediate move to an average thirty-five-hour week, and a further progressive reduction to thirty hours a week by the beginning of the next century.

Clearly this notion of work sharing has nothing to do with ideas about unemployment sharing and spread of casual work (affecting women in the service sector primarily), spuriously called 'work sharing' and peddled by certain politicians of both Left and Right. This share-out of unemployment merely amounts to a generalization of part-time and part-wage jobs – where people already paid less than the minimum wage have to content themselves with a half-job and a half-wage. What I am proposing is a reduction in normal working time but with normal remuneration – thus allowing, for example, a single mother to live properly.

Moreover, this work sharing will only be accepted by the majority already in work (since it implies some redistribution of income to be effective) if in actual experience it is a *growth of free time*, of an enhanced free time. This is a prerequisite of *autonomy*: a society of free individuals is one where they have free time, as we have known since Aristotle. We need free time for civic life, to develop our autonomous activities.. We need free time to consume what we have already bought: to listen to music, read books, indulge in sport or photography. We need free time above all for friendship and love.

Creating a society which gauges progress by the growth of free time more than by the accumulation of wealth is an imperative stemming from *responsibility* – the crisis of waste matter and climate change through the greenhouse effect is merely the consequence of a model of the indefinite growth of mass consumption.

Choices such as these need basic *ground rules*. They need political action to regulate, tax and ban harmful activities, and to co-ordinate a reduction of working time sufficient for massive job creation; diplomatic action to impose ecological and social conditions on free trade, and to prevent these fine imperatives from being swept aside by the perversity of worldwide competition; a huge effort of solidarity with the Third World, so that it does not have to 'make the best of what it has'.

Concerning reduction of working time, the Greens in Europe, and all trade union movements in Western Europe, have proposed the immediate reduction of the working week to an average of thirty-five hours, and ecologists are also in favour of all forms of the voluntary 'regrouping' of free time by calculating the reduction on a yearly basis, and possible sabbatical years. In France, such a move from the present thirty-nine-hour working week would, according to econometrists,[5] save around 2 million jobs over three years. Loss of pay could be offset by 70 per cent (i.e. $37\frac{3}{4}$ hours' pay for thirty-five hours' work) *on average*, without jeopardizing the profitability or competitiveness of firms. Why is this? Because on the one hand it is a known fact, proved by statistics, that a 2 per cent drop in working hours leads to only a 1 per cent (i.e. half as much) fall in actual work done. This is because the marginal hours of work are the least productive, as well as the most dangerous in terms of accidents at work. This increased productivity through reduction of working time itself explains why the reduction does not free up as many jobs as a fixed formula might indicate, but only half as many. However, it does mean that some of the hours not worked can be paid for. On the other hand, 2 million unemployed people back in work would reduce the welfare payments bill and increase the numbers paying contributions – provided *all* employers did the same. In this way, some of the 'indirect cost' of unemployment could be released into direct pay – if the reduction in hours of work is a large one.

A huge reduction in hours worked, with only partial loss of pay, is therefore possible only if legislation (or multi-sector collective agreement in countries where this has applied) gives the signal. This is the *absolute* condition for firms launching into reducing worktime to be certain their competitors will do the same. It is the condition for a drop in unemployment to be large and predictable enough to allow a reduction in social welfare contributions. This simple operation of game theory is forgotten in France by those who since 1982 have been calling for a 'negotiated firm-by-firm reduction', with the result, now obvious, that since 1982 each employer has been waiting for somebody else to start the ball rolling!

A legislative framework for a reduction does not mean there should be no negotiation within firms on the details of adjustment, in line with a timetable fixing the total overtime allowed as an interim measure.[6] Legislation needs to establish the collective context for individual adjustments.

For the reduction to work properly (though experience in Germany shows it may not be necessary – German workers already work 100 hours a year fewer than their French counterparts, and many were on thirty-five hours or less in 1994), it would be better co-ordinated at the real macroeconomic level – that is, Europe. Greens in the European Parliament have been fighting for this for years; but the Single Act, and then the Treaty of Maastricht, made sure they excluded social matters from the European democratic arena. This is why the Greens, in the name of social Europe, were opposed to agreements increasing the free movement of capital and promoting the unfortunate rivalry of workers. Neither are they in favour of treaties which will have nothing to do with the sustainable development of the Community's territory, favouring instead those countries with the least strict environmental rules.

The final point is that any non-loss of wages for working fewer hours should not be uniform, since it is already difficult to live on the minimum wage in urban areas. The French Greens' suggestion is that, within the overall framework, mentioned above, of a 70 per cent offset (of wages lost through reduced hours), there should be no loss of pay up to median wage (about twice the minimum wage in France), and a progressive loss above that level. This 'graduated clawback' could be done by collective negotiation, an increase in the minimum hourly rate or through the tax system. The Greens are proposing a tax on income dependent on the size of pay differentials within the firm. This is merely a suggestion, and what counts is the end result – a return to lower pay differentials, such as exist in Germany, or such as existed in France in 1982, before ten years of socialism introduced excessive inequalities.

A multiple attack on unemployment

The thirty-five-hour week, as I have said, is primarily a way of fighting unemployment and social exclusion. However, in France, this would be only a part of the solution (jobs for 2 million out of 4 or 5 million really unemployed). Since the reduction in working time is effective against unemployment only if accompanied by some redistribution of income, we must be careful not to set aims which, as a single package, are too ambitious (such as 'thirty hours now!'), and would raise the problem of finding immediate jobs for 3 million unemployed.

We must therefore look to other solutions; when it comes to unemployment, *there is no panacea*, and different angles of attack have to be tried. I have already mentioned one approach – work techniques which are more intensive (in the areas of agriculture or energy) but less destructive of the environment, and the development of ecological activities such as the improvement of neighbourhoods and recycling. Ecologists are not against all growth in activity, only unsustainable growth.

This leads us to the inescapable question of economic recovery. Why in fact should we not return to the old 1960s strategy of full employment, and promote recovery of economic activity through a policy of major public works, thus creating jobs? Ever since my first book on the economic policies of the Left,[7] and in everything I have contributed since then, I have in fact been calling for a measure of recovery, a 'selective recovery'. However, we need to be clear about its conditions and objectives.

First, there are two constraints on recovery – an investment constraint from lack of money in the coffers of firms and government, and the 'external constraint', i.e. the problem of the national balance of trade. The first constraint means that there has to be a careful choice of particular sectors for recovery (those where the most jobs would be created for each franc invested), and the second constraint raises the problem of the competitiveness of national goods.

This point leads us in turn to the debate about the 'strong currency'.

Since the famous U-turn of 1983, when the socialist government in France chose to sacrifice its social policy on the altar of the strong franc, I have called for devaluation, and been scoffed at by those 'competent' people responsible for 3 million unemployed. Their argument has been that a currency overvalued against that of its competitors will oblige firms to hold down prices and go flat out for productivity, in order to compete from a healthy base. In other words, 'competitive disinflation'.

By 1991–2, this strategy seemed finally to have succeeded, not on the jobs front, but at least with regard to the trade balance, which was back in surplus. However, a careful look at the facts confirms the dangers of an overvalued currency. The reason why French goods had become once again competitive was that all France's neighbours were following an unreasonable policy of overvaluation. Italy, Spain, the United Kingdom, with inflation higher than in France, were clinging to an exchange rate which was too high, and Germany was paying for reunification by inflation. Then everything blew up in September 1992: Italy, Spain and the United Kingdom devalued, and Germany became bogged down in stagnation. The markets of France's trading partners contracted, while their exports became more competitive.

A policy of an over valued franc, such as the present (1995) one is a policy of import subsidy, a policy which penalizes exports. Even worse – since the franc is permanently under attack (being overvalued), high interest rates are needed to 'reward' foreigners willing to hold francs. This policy in its turn inhibits the ability to finance investment, in particular in the ecological and social fields (rational use of energy, public transport, housing).

It is with bitter irony that nowadays I hear one-time orthodox voices, on the Left and the Right, calling for economic recovery . . . and devaluation. Some even refer to recent writing by economists close to the Clinton camp who, under the name of 'endogenous growth', are reinventing the wheel set in motion by Roosevelt before the war: we must spend money on major public works which create jobs in the short term and help regional development. Elementary, my dear Watson!

But at least spare us more white elephants, greedy for land and capital. Refurbish the stock of affordable housing if we must; by all means build well-insulated apartment blocks which are pleasant to live in; modernize public transport, fine. But spare us a profusion of half-deserted motorways, or a Rhine–Rhône canal as useless as it is disastrous for the ecology of the Jura region. Recovery in the construction and public works sector is very effective in creating jobs and does not suck in imports; but we must be very ecologically and financially selective when it comes to choosing which works to proceed with.

Finally, let us not indulge in dreams. Unemployment will not fall overnight. Halving the unemployment rate within one parliament would already be an achievement.

Another battle to fight is that of the social reintegration of those unemployed people for whom the market will not be able to find work. What is at stake is a 'third sector' between private and public sector – a sector of co-operatives, intermediate agencies and intermediate firms, subsidized on a permanent basis (as unemployed people are), and exempt from taxes and welfare contributions (as unemployed people are), and therefore not costing society a penny more, but able to provide services for it at very low prices while giving its workers a normal wage and a proper status. A sector of social utility, dedicated to performing certain tasks for private individuals and to restoring the environment, self-managed, in a contractual relationship with the end-user. In other words, give a proper rate of pay to marginalized people to do something useful, and thereby to recover social recognition, rather than keeping them as receivers of welfare benefits.

A third sector such as this could eventually number a million people at any one time. More than a (necessary) reform of state funding of unemployment, we need to move from the welfare state to the welfare community.

Tax reform

I have already referred briefly to the ecologist approach to the tax system – that it should be used proactively to bring about new patterns of behaviour, not only as a financial pump. True, 'a good tax is an old tax', but old taxes in new situations, with new imperatives, produce absurd results – when French local government was decentralized, the old local tax system meant that the richer a local authority was, the less it taxed firms and households, and vice versa.

For these reasons, Greens are in favour of a major reform of the tax system. The most unexpected, and the most criticized, proposal is *an end to taxation of company profits*. Yes, really! After all, why penalize a firm's economic efficiency as such? Income from capital, i.e. *income accruing to its owners*, ought to contribute to collective needs by a supplement on the income tax of individuals, without any deduction or, of course, tax credit. This does not mean that companies will pay significantly less in tax, but they will pay taxes which are more 'intelligent', and which encourage more ecological behaviour. An 'ecotax' on energy consumption and carbon gas emissions, which Brussels is proposing in order to counter the greenhouse effect (of the order of ten dollars per barrel of oil equivalent), will offset most of what is lost by ending taxes on profits.

Even more radical are Green proposals for reforming personal taxation, which currently in France is particularly unfair. Social welfare (national insurance) contributions constitute the greater part but are levied only on earned income. The next most important tax, VAT, is levied on all spending, by rich and poor alike, and on spending from earned and unearned income alike. VAT is usually regarded as an unfair tax, less progressive than income tax; but it is much fairer than social welfare contributions, in that it is levied on spending from *all* income sources. True, the consumption share in income falls when income increases, but this can be offset by fine-tuning VAT, with a higher rate for luxury items or those which are harmful to the environment. Finally, income tax itself constitutes the smallest part. It is highly progressive, in that the rate increases with income, but there are significant tax allowances on unearned income.

The French Greens' proposal is a gradual switch to financing family welfare benefits from income tax, and sick pay from VAT. Only retirement benefit contributions would stay as a levy on earned income, as a kind of personal saving. But it has to be realized that retirement benefit contributions are set to go on rising; if people live longer and work less, a greater proportion of earned income will inevitably be needed to finance retirement.

In any event, the redistributive effect of this reform will be enormous, in favour of those on earned income, since income from other sources (particularly from capital) will be more highly taxed. The reason why not all tax take will be moved to income tax is that it would be too much at one time, even during the lifetime of one parliament. In France, the Green proposal already involves the doubling of VAT and a large increase in direct income tax.

These switches will have no impact on general price levels and, if tax is taken at source, taxpayers will hardly notice the change. Companies will pay money to the tax authorities, who will transfer to the social welfare funds a proportion of what firms used to pay directly to these funds. An increase in VAT raises no problems in the context of the European Union, since VAT is levied at the frontiers; this will apply at least until 1996, and harmonization of rates is well into the future. This was really why VAT was invented, and it represents a major advantage – VAT is not paid on exported goods. When uniform VAT rates are looked at again in 1996, this model could be adopted for the whole of Europe, since Europe will need to protect itself from competition from countries without social security systems.

Changing scale

Once again it is clear that social and ecological progress is only really possible when taxation, collective agreements and legislation apply to the same territorial area as that of the economic activity. Nowadays 'globalization' is the icing on the cake of conservatism: 'we are powerless, world markets are supreme, we can do nothing.' Political ecology rejects this surrender, and fights it in two ways:

By reducing the geographical scale of economic channels: Greens favour regional partnership, 'short circuits' between producers and consumers, through agreements with distributors. They are in favour of taxing long-distance transport etc.

More importantly, by increasing the scale of democracy; by giving Europe its missing ecological, fiscal and social dimensions; by strengthening or establishing transnational regulatory bodies to introduce ecological and social clauses into free-trade mechanisms.

This is what the Greens are fighting for in the European Parliament, an institution largely ignored by the Treaty of Maastricht, which short-circuits democracy at the European level.

However, a retreat on this front is not inevitable; a new economic revolution is in train, even more significant than the one which Keynesianism and social democracy imposed on capitalism fifty years ago, as significant no doubt as the late medieval enclosure movement which divided fields up between efficient farmers. The conservatism of the defenders of the old productivist model may lead to an 'environment war'. Ecologists believe that the revolution of the twenty-first century must bring about an economic model which nature can sustain, because it is based on human solidarity.

PART II

International and Worldwide Perspectives

6

From Garden to Planet

As soon as political ecology begins to contemplate the geographical scale of its action, it is torn between two imperatives, or rather two contradictory aspirations. On the one hand, how can one possibly not be overwhelmed by a tremendous feeling of responsibility for this fragile vessel lauched into the universe – Earth? It is a marvellous blue bubble which our lack of consciousness threatens to swamp with atomic mushroom clouds, deprive of its protective ozone layer, and foul up with greenhouse gas emissions which in coming decades will change climates, disrupt ocean currents and raise sea levels. With such risks to the planet, any consciousness of the 'global' would readily lead to calls for a world order, political schemes of regulation on a planetary scale, or indeed world government.

On the other hand, the most immediate ecologist aspiration is to regain control of the much nearer bubble – the world outside our front door or garden gate, shared with a living community of people whom we know, whether we like or dislike them, and with whom we can debate and reach compromises. We are condemned to live with one another in this local bubble; but this bubble, our 'environment' (since 'environment' means 'surroundings'), the government of which ought to be the expression of the most direct form of democracy, escapes from our grasp, a mere baby's rattle

shaken and battered by paramount forces and external giants
– the winds of global competition, the arbitrary workings of
nation-states, or superstates like the European administration in Brussels.

Think globally, act locally

It is by reference to this maxim – surely indeed accurate and
always valid – that ecologists have tried to resolve the contradiction. Let us have a closer look at it.

Act locally: this is the wish to be in charge of one's environment. Above all, the assertion of a right, against
centralism, against the totalitarianism of the nation-state and
world markets; it expresses a wish to think and act for oneself, at one's own level, without delegation or subordination to an external Great Genius; it is the demand for
regionalization, even municipalization, of political power.
But it is also consciousness of *duties* and responsibilities – we
act locally because there is no excuse not to do so, or not to
do so properly; locally, we can measure the cost to neighbours of moving around in our common bubble. If one beat
of a butterfly's wing is a co-determinant of wind systems over
the whole planet in non-linear aerodynamics, then there is all
the more reason for us to think that every car journey we
make contributes to global warming, rising sea levels in the
Gulf of Bengal and further desertification of the Sahel.

Think globally: because thoughts of the global bring us to
this local responsibilty; because we must learn to move away
from the compromises of our local bubble to take stock of
the damage to our global bubble; because the slogan of ecol-

ogy is not 'not in my back yard'; because political ecology adopts and makes its own the slogans of basic humanism, from Terence and Dostoyevsky to Emmanuel Levinas and Hans Jonas: 'I am a human being, and everything human is my business', 'we are all responsible for everything and to everybody, and myself in particular'; because responsibility cannot be based other than on *knowledge* – knowledge of other specific bubbles such as the villages of the *seringueros* of the Amazon, the villages of Burkina Faso and Bangladesh, the shanty towns of Lima, or the refugee camps in Gaza. Knowledge also of the many links between all the bubbles – links through debt as well as through cries of hatred, through raw material prices and through polluting gas emissions.

If all men and women had this marvellous knowledge, if their soul and spirit took account of the most far-reaching consequences of every act, if their love of others and of nature inspired every one of their actions, there would be no need at all to go beyond the maxim 'think globally, act locally.'

But this is the point: human beings are not perfect. They do not even see the consequences of their innumerable trivial acts. What possible effect has five tonnes of carbon emitted each year into the huge expanse of the atmosphere? But when 250 million people in the United States do the same, this amounts to 250 million criminals. And when they find out what they are doing, will they pay any attention? 'Our lifestyle is not negotiable', asserted President Bush in the Rio negotiations. It is not even clear that this kind of cynicism cost him re-election.

Human beings are cynical and selfish; their short-sightedness is merely the blindness of people refusing to see.

This is the basis for arguing the need for laws. And since they have to be prevented from causing harm globally, what we need is global laws. Even if we thought that human beings are perfectible, the 'precautionary principle' leads political ecology to act, prudently and realistically, as if they were not. If we need to act globally, they need to be convinced, on the ground, by local compromises, to accept global laws. *Act globally, think locally*: this also must be the slogan of *Realökologie*.

Act globally, think locally

Act globally: this involves establishing the rules of a higher order (higher than local bubbles), and acquiring the means to ensure that they are applied. It is a matter of getting rid of unintended composition effects, preventing bad practices which may be advantageous in local terms, but taken together can be disastrous for the whole, or for other localities. Fix minimum wage rates or maximum working hours, establish maximum pollution levels, stabilize raw material prices; in other words regulate the free play of selfishness and competition in world markets, and promote practices which are mutually advantageous.

Think locally: this means appreciating the difficulties of applying locally a global rule, however advantageous it is for everybody in the long term (especially for future generations who can neither vote nor demonstrate), when it may be against everybody's freedom and everybody's immediate interest, and even against locally agreed compromises. It involves thinking about the conditions of the *legitimacy* of laws and governments – a legitimacy which is sometimes imposed globally ('thou shalt not kill'), but which vanishes in the mists of speculation and challenge: 'Why should *I* limit my consumption when others will carry on consuming, all for something uncertain and remote?'[1]

It is a miracle that human beings spontaneously obey laws without being forced. Eighteenth-century philosophy (the social contract) and the more demanding social contract of 'responsibility ecologists' such as Hans Jonas and Michel Serres, both try to bring about this miracle by persuasion and incantation. In reality, the miracle has historically only been achieved in two ways – religion and the nation.

Religions are symbolic forces progressively transformed into internalized responsibility. We regard the Ten Commandments as 'natural', but their effectiveness was for a long time based on fear of hell and divine retribution. Even nowadays, secularized Christian morality has to lean on secular laws and punishments, whereas Catholicism is somewhat outdated by comparison with the most elevated forms of secular morality: it does not accept the separation of sexual love and reproduction, it tolerates the death penalty, and rejects the basic equality of men and women. We can conceive of an ecologist morality for modern times, but not a religion for modern times, at least not one with the 'force of law'.

The nation is that large bubble in which we obey laws even if we disagree with them, even if we are part of the minority which did not vote for them. We are prepared to wait for them to be amended, we accept the will of other people because we internalize a common destiny with tens of millions of men and women whom we will never meet, who are not our 'neighbours' or our immediate 'environment', but with whom we share a past of sacrifices, values and historically constructed habits, and a present consisting of hopes. 'The nation', as Ernest Renan said, 'is a plebiscite every day – about the choice of living together.' At the present time, of all legitimated bubbles, it is the most elevated.

However, in the face of competition on the world market, of ecological dangers to the planet, this bubble is already too small, and too often based on the hatred of other bubbles. The idea of the nation, imposing limitations on the demands of its inhabitants, soon turns into nationalism, involving denial of rights to 'those who do not belong', hatred of others . . . To act globally and think locally is to establish rules and supranational authorities which have the legitimacy of the nation; gradually to bring local communities (of which the most all-encompassing are for the time being nations) to a consciousness of the common destiny of humankind, of common values, of common needs, of superior mutual advantages; and to act politically and diplomatically for international codification of rules which local majorities are prepared to accept.

This is where the Treaty of Maastricht went wrong – it delegated to national executives and the Brussels technocracy the task of building the 'common European home'. Without a feeling of belonging to a Europe which establishes everyone's rights and duties, without the approval of a directly elected constituent European Parliament, laws emanating from Brussels are bound to be seen as foreign (even to Belgians!). For instance, by the end of 1992, we saw the most fervent supporters of Maastricht opposing an EEC–USA agreement within GATT on the grounds that it was not in the interests of most small farmers in France![2]

Europe can only come about in a different way: through the gradual establishment of institutions guaranteeing social welfare and fostering ecological responsibility, leaving to the local level (municipalities, regions or nations), that is, to 'bubbles' accessible through democratic practice, the bulk of power over everyday matters.

As for the world level, the reason for the minimal success of the Rio Conference was, apart from the cynicism of the Bush administration, that countries and peoples in the South did not want a 'world ecological authority' imposing its policy on them, like the UN Security Council or the International Monetary Fund.

The peoples of the South are prepared to accept an authority which would guarantee human rights, protect the rights of nature and future generations without sacrificing the right of *all* living humans to a decent life. This authority at the present time would be a 'judicial' one, and the International Court in The Hague could well fit the bill. It would have the right to hear plaintiffs, including NGOs, it would be able to condemn states violating human rights and the rights of nature as universally recognized. It may not have for some time the means to enforce its judgements. But it would be the beginning of worldwide legitimacy. It would at least be a start . . .

This aim of a new world order, more socially just and more ecologically sustainable, is an extension of what the old Left called 'internationalism'. However, though Green globalism is even more ambitious (in that it involves the rights of future generations), in a sense it is also more modest. The old internationalism was not without its faults.

7

A Modest Internationalism

For a long time, the Left in Europe approached the question of its relationship with the peoples of other continents on the basis of a few simple ideas.[1] Above all, its universalist duty was to help them. But help them to do what? To be like itself, like the Europe of its dreams, or what it dreamed Europe should be like. In effect, there was only one road to progress; and non-European peoples were clearly not on this road, in that they were dominated, militarily and politically. Help could come only from the dominators.

The civilized Left had nothing to learn from these barbarians. Even when it pretended to idolize the 'noble savage', it merely manufactured fictions, projecting its dreams on to phantom peoples. This tradition, which goes back at least as far as Voltaire, continued up to the writings of certain contemporary anthropologists, such as Margaret Mead and Marshall Sahlins. There was a vague wish to recognize 'otherness', but only to the extent that it indicated a possible line of progress for us in Europe. It was an unworldly intuition of progress, in other words, which only Europe (or its elder daughter, North America, and then a rival younger daughter, the Soviet Union) could make universal, and then re-export, duly stamped with rationality, to backward peoples.

Immodest internationalism

The idea was therefore to help; but we were also well aware that in reality, the Europe of Christianity, progress and Enlightenment was not really helping poor savages. The fact was that European colonizers were unworthy of Europe – unworthy Christians, for the Jesuits of Paraguay, and unworthy republicans, for Victor Hugo. Real Europe pillaged, raped and exploited, whereas ideal Europe helped.

Helped to do what? To be like us; to participate in our progress; to share our values; to apply our resources. Europe had the technology, which is why it was dominant. Technology meant the growth of welfare, and it was this that counted. Europe's idea of progress was the maximization of individual welfare. To which the Left added a rider: the welfare of *all* individuals. The Left had an instrument for this – the state, representing the interests of all against the blinkered selfishness of individuals.

The Left in Europe met again its old anti-progress adversaries in Africa and Asia, and among the American Indians – heads of families, native chiefs, landowners. The way to overcome them was to do away with existing social relationships, generalize the principles of 1789, re-establish individual rights outside Europe under the benevolent supervision of the democratic state.

The more radical wing of the European Left knew, of course, that 1789 had not fulfilled its promises. At the heart of Europe, the proletariat represented the negation of human rights. Europe was not the future of humanity, but a dead-end – not because of rectifiable mistakes by despotic minorities, but because of structural defects in the principles of 1789. One of the now universal rights of individuals was the right to private property; this not only put paid to the idea of community, but also potentially split society right down the middle – between those who were able to increase their possessions and those whose assets were reduced, initially by some chance happening (affecting individual or community), and then by the mechanism of capitalist accumulation. Marx's *Communist Manifesto* and his *Capital* denounced this implacable mechanism, seeing in it both the basis of European power (increase in productive forces brought about by capitalist accumulation) and the promise of a subsequent reversal – takeover of the exploiters for the benefit of the community.

Even in the most radical critique of European progress, therefore, it was not really a question of a dead-end. Despite odd warnings from Marx himself, capitalism seemed to be a valley of tears, but on balance the end result would be positive. Progress in European terms (individual enrichment through the unconditional development of productive forces) was not challenged. The only challenge was to obstacles which capitalist private property imposed on this development. The Second, Third and even the Fourth Internationals shared in this progressive creed of a 'conquering bourgeoisie'.

From then on, the European Left was able with impunity to divide over the question of 'backward' peoples. The 'moderates' (or 'republicans', as they could be termed) mechanically transferred the ideas of 1789 into what came to be called the 'Third World' and saw no problem in installing a capitalist system there, provided it had a human face; opposing them, there appeared radicals, whose aim was not to help others become like us, but rather to help them *not* become like us, that is, *not* to adopt a capitalist system. However, their way of helping others not to become as Europe was at that time, was to help them become what they thought it could be: a socialist system.

In other words, the radical approach was to try to miss out the capitalist stage. All depended on the interpretation of a basic premise: the difficulty in developing, from the turn of the twentieth century, an authentic capitalism. Theories of imperialism, and then of dependency, transformed the basic premise behind this difficulty into a conclusion that it was impossible – there had been a capitalist path to a shining future, but such a path was no longer available, since it was at present blocked by advanced capitalisms which were close to socialism. On this basis, any struggle for independence was at the same time a struggle against capitalism and a struggle for socialism. It could still be disputed (Stalin versus Trotsky versus Mao . . .) whether or not the transition to socialism needed a stage of 'national capitalism', but this in any event was under the control of a party with socialist objectives.

Behind these byzantine quarrels about an uninterrupted and/or stage-by-stage revolution, there was indeed one fundamental point of agreement: the transition to socialism implied the unification of social structures in the form of the wage-earning class (even as co-operatives) and under the direction of the state. Here again, a counter-argument could be found in Marx's final misgivings (his letter to Vera Zassulich talks of a direct transition from Russian peasant society to socialism), the final attempts of Bukharin, or the community-style experiments of Che Guevara or Mao Zedong. These, however, do not contradict the general trend: behind the attempt to help others not to be the same as us was the dream of helping them to be what we wanted to be, by quick fixes but using the same paradigm of progress.

Halfway through the twentieth century, the European Left was imposing on Left movements in the Third World the triptych of growth of productive forces, wage-earning class, state.

This 'help' by the Left in Europe cost the new nations of the Third World untold sacrifices and untold wastage – how many blast furnaces paid for by the sweat of peasants, or rolling mills which crushed the hands of young workers, were left to rust on the banks of 'socialist transition'! How many 'models' (poles of development, industrializing sectors and so on) did intellectuals of the European Left sell to the peoples of Africa and Asia, with the only tangible result of making them buy goods and relations of production from the northern part of the Western world!

Forty years on, we need to sound the retreat. A quick fix is impossible. All people's democracies, all systems of socialism in Africa or Asia, applying criteria common to both the conquering bourgeoisie and internationalists, have performed markedly less well than those Third World countries which have gone furthest in acculturation to capitalism – the 'little dragons' of Asia. From Poland to China, the dream is no longer of socialism, nor even of Sweden, but of Korea; and the example of Finland suggests that Korea is the most direct way to Sweden. The surest way to development, according to European criteria of progress, seems once more to be the valley of tears of capitalism.

The failure of 'development'

We have to distinguish different levels of causality in this disturbing failure.

The first lesson immediately apparent is that there is no single development, but only *models* of development. Writers who nowadays condemn development because it has been transplanted without success[2] are simply making the same mistake as those who in the past (often the same people) wanted to impose (or 'suggest') their own ideas of development as a model. The prime obstacle to importing the ways and methods of European progress was the lack of a society 'over there' ready to commit itself fully, to 'play the game' of this model of progress. Productive forces, wage-earning class and state were heaped in an inorganic jumble on recalcitrant communities. Long-standing social relationships (no more 'natural' than European ones) were smashed by force of arms, or crushed by competition, or diluted in a semi-acculturation which produced a society of down-and-outs. New 'European' relationships did not 'take' as a development model, as technological matrix, as regime of accumulation, as mode of regulation, since they were not organized as a 'societal paradigm', a model of life in society, a promise of an ideal of progress accepted and desired by everybody.[3] At best, individuals, robbed of their ties and dreams, were able to cling to the floating wreckage of an imported modernity: ridiculous gadgets of the consumer society for some, grotesque baubles of state power for others. Too little to constitute a system and lifestyle (except in East Asia), too much to be able to find happiness in the ruins of a lost community.

Let us, however, not forget dependency. This failed 'development' was not wasted for everybody. Traders and employers in the North were able to cash in on it. But let us beware of seeing 'dependency' as the cause of the failure. Some countries steered clear of dependency, but still failed; others

were full participants in interdependence, and succeeded . . .
by going down the road of capitalist development.[4]

This is the whole point: capitalist development in all its
variants, this very basic way of being European, this way in
which Hong Kong has become another Venice, this ideal of
progress that the old European Left still clings to, is, quite
apart from its failure to transplant, sick in its native soil. Or,
as it is described, 'in crisis'; but not just in economic crisis.
If this were the only problem, capitalism would eventually
come up with a new development model. It will in the end
find one; it may already have found one. But I do not think
so, and it can hardly hope to find one by pursuing something
that the old Left might recognize as 'progress'. Capitalism is
progressing, of course, but on the ruins of former hopes.
Productive forces are leading us to ecological catastrophe.
Changes in the wage-earning groups are destroying communities of wage-earners. The state, challenged by new social movements, overwhelmed by new trends in capitalism,
has dropped the sceptre of the future. The European Left has
to make a choice – either to go along with capitalism and stop
being the Left, or to reinvent progress and stop being the old
Left.

Let me say it again, at the risk of boring people by state-
ments which lack even the virtue of being iconoclastic. The
old Left in Europe caught on to a *capitalist* ideal of progress
– more production, more consumption, more state intervention. It reached its peak – social democracy – with the Fordist
compromise, imposing on capitalism itself a development
model which in effect applied this maxim. Nowadays, when
the compromise is shattered on the capitalist side, when the
state can no longer guarantee the distribution of the 'dividends of progress', when ecological constraints demanded by

Green activists prevent universal application of the growth model and threaten its survival even in 'advanced' countries, the old Left is silent and disoriented, not just in the Third World, but in Europe itself.

Rethinking internationalism

An alternative to the old Left – the alternative such as has developed since 1968 (the first world-scale mass movement against the 'old world' and its old Left) has been defining itself, as I said earlier, in relation to three themes which constitute the touchstone for any kind of 'progress' and any democratic politics: autonomy of individuals and groups, solidarity between individuals and groups, ecological responsibility as the guiding principle of relationships between society, the product of its activities and its environment.

In chapter 5, I suggested the principal characteristics of a development model which applied these principles in Europe and any other developed capitalist country. But what of solidarity with less developed countries? What kind of 'internationalism' does the alternative propose? The answer is that it has to be *a modest internationalism*. Since it is clear that one cannot define for somebody else what kind of happiness they ought to have, and since autonomy implies freedom for each community to establish its ideal of progress, tomorrow's internationalism has got to be minimalist. It should aim to establish a world order favouring the greatest freedom of choice for communities (the principle of *maximal variability*). This 'neutrality' does not, however, mean passivity: it must aim to ensure everywhere a basic set of human rights (the principle of *minimal universalism*). Finally the alternative internationalism must recognize that it has as much to learn from others' development models as from its own genius, and that problems of co-operation with others spring not only from inconsistencies and deficiencies on the part of others, but also from the intrinsic limitations of one's own development model. Clearly, 'modest' internationalism is a *self-demanding* internationalism!

I mentioned the principle of maximal variability. Unlike those who praise the 'convergence of political systems' and the 'end of history', modest internationalism believes that historical experimentation never stops, that every community has the right to explore new ways for humankind, on the basis of its own traditions and its particular aspirations. Unlike the arrogance of the IMF and the World Bank, modest internationalism is not sure that there exist generally applicable remedies, and in any case not those of economic liberals:

because economic liberalism, which has brought neither justice nor well-being to the United States is hardly likely to be appropriate for communities which start off with fewer natural advantages;

because macroeconomic logic shows that everybody trying to get the better of everybody else can only lead to a worse result than a non-aggressive negotiated order, giving everyone the largest possible degree of freedom.

The logic of the uncontrolled free market is in fact easy to understand. As in the 'prisoner's dilemma', where a prison governor organizes rivalry among prisoners for his or her own benefit, the present economic order organizes for the benefit of creditor states the rivalry of debtor countries, obliging them to 'pull out all stops', socially and ecologically, to repay debts through export earnings. The abolition of Third World debt is the first thing to do to give back to each debtor nation a range of choice. Of course, clearing debts will in no way solve the internal problems of the country in question; but it will open up the *possibility*. It is not up to the IMF, nor the World Bank, nor ecologists, nor the European Left to decide on behalf of an African country whether its ideal should be a social-democratized Korea or a community based on villages. On the other hand, the experience of the Sudan, on which the window of democracy closed after a period of a few months under the pressure of debt manipulated by the World Bank, shows how pitiful dreams of democracy can be when their economic realization is impossible.

However, despite its modesty, the new internationalism cannot limit itself merely to getting rid of a dead weight from the past. It must also aim to establish rules for the future, based on the principle of maximal variability, which itself articulates the principle of autonomy, and which could be once again reformulated: 'the freedom of every community stops where that of others begins.' It is not therefore a matter of re-engaging the same ill-fitting mechanisms. A country whose ecological and social behaviour could affect the freedom of others to keep their own equilibria should not be allowed to put pressure on these countries through its superior competitiveness. Social and ecological clauses on free trade, arbitrated by international institutions, are therefore necessary to stop these new kinds of dumping – minimal rules about the conditions of exploitation of workers, of nature, and so on. This is why ecologists were so opposed to the ultra-liberals in the GATT negotiations.

We should not hide the frightening complexity of the problems raised by all this framework of rules. Too stringent standards would exclude from international trade certain low-productivity countries, even though such standards would represent considerable progress for these countries. To be just, common rules should be dynamically differentiated. It is not a matter of saying that all countries should adopt the same minimum hourly wage rate, or that all should reduce their greenhouse gas emissions. It must be recognized that not all start from the same position: lower wage rates in a low-productivity country do not have unfair effects on international competition, and it is acceptable for a country which increases its standard of living also to add initially to the greenhouse effect. However, common rules should aim gradually to harmonize social and ecological standards, and first to guarantee workers' rights worldwide. The notion of 'common rules' immediately highlights the *minimal universalism* of our modest internationalism, which articulates the principle of solidarity.

Though modest, the new internationalism is not neutral. It argues that there is a common basic set of human values, and fights for their realization. It does not make relativism into an absolute value. It is not so naive as to believe in innate goodness, in the non-contradictory nature of human communities. Although it refrains from imposing on others its conception of 'human', it is in solidarity with people among these others who fight against inhumanity.

We see here the paradoxes of the debate in France about one aspect of North–South relations – treatment of immigrant communities. For a long time, the Left fought against inequality using an assimilation approach – let foreigners become like us, and they will be our equals. Recognition of the 'right to be different' threw into crisis this strangely racist kind of anti-racism. However, 'equality through difference', though acceptable as a slogan, raises tremendous practical difficulties. For example, a secular education system (a perfect example of the *maximal universalism* of the old Left) is now challenged by the introduction into the French education system of cultural traits which are 'different', yet have – from the secular viewpoint – oppressive connotations. I am referring to the debate started in autumn 1989 on whether school authorities could ban the wearing of the Islamic headscarf. Of course, if a secular system means toleration of all, respect for community autonomy and application of the principle of maximum variability, it is scandalous to forbid the expression of 'Muslim characteristics' in an education system supposed to be secular but in fact deeply influenced, even down to details of its term times, by the demands of Catholic liturgy.

Let us not be disingenuous, however. The Islamic headscarf denotes a patriarchal system with other much less acceptable 'community characteristics' such as arranged marriage. Universalism comes back to its rights when it asserts the freedom of women to choose their destiny. Women teachers in France are well aware of this when they organize escape networks for their fifteen-year-old Muslim female students, having themselves had to fight in their own adolescence against their own alienation and that of their sisters, in the face of a dominant religion and state laws which denied them rights over their own bodies.

Although the principle of maximum variability is a matter of national laws or international regulations establishing what is permitted and what is forbidden (the right to wear or not wear a headscarf in class, the right to use or not use contraception), minimum universalism needs to be ultra-modest in the use of legal sanctions. Forbidding arranged marriages, or excision, or infibulation may well be covered by the principle of variability (*possibilities* are being left open for young females, and they are not being prevented from accepting a position of alienation later) but only from the point of view of a community which is partly disalienated (at least in this respect). In a community without corresponding values (which, it must be remembered, are recent achievements even in the North), even the victims of such practices might regard an imposed disalienation as a scandal or an attack on them. The activism of conviction is in this case the only unequivocal approach to adopt. It rests on an active solidarity, *to a large degree non-governmental*, between men and women who, in the North and in the South, share the values of minimum universalism, values reasonably well represented by the Universal Declaration of Human Rights, to which has now been added the recognition of specific rights of women and children.

Faced with tremendous threats to these rights, even if only the right to life, of necessity encompassing future generations, the tasks of minimum universalism are far from insignificant. Let us look, for example, at the population problem. Europe has played havoc with the human ecology of Africa, smashing development models which were ecologically sustainable for centuries. The present demographic explosion, representing a demographic transition not yet over, is strictly unsustainable, given the technology, property relations and urban–rural price systems obtaining throughout most of Africa. Agronomists such as René Dumont argue convincingly that it will never be sustainable, even with exclusively economic reforms. The Earth has never promised that it would tolerate any human density, in return for a bit of good will! Aids may play for Africa the role of the Black Death in fourteenth-century feudal Europe – the uncontrolled solution of an ecological-social-economic-demographic crisis.

The principle of solidarity or minimum universalism deprives ecologists and the European Left of any cause for satisfaction. Saving Africa will be expensive. It will involve Africans in a cultural sea-change in gender relationships, and fundamental agrarian reforms, which Europeans cannot impose, but which they can help to bring about.[5] It will need huge resource transfers, regarded as fair by the African conception of community laws and obligations; what is clear is that African communities have stored up in their memory, from the slave trade to colonial forced labour, huge potential rights over the present assets of Europe . . .

We now look at the third aspect of modest internationalism: *self-demandingness*, the articulation in the international context of the principle of ecological sustainability. The European ecologist alternative must recognize that 'backward peoples' have had, and often still have, much more respect for the common heritage of humanity than the old Left, which inculcated in them its own idea of progress; that these 'backward communities' were often aware that human beings belong to nature rather than the opposite; that the future of humankind and this planet is threatened more by the Stalinist and social democratic madnesses of the 1950s to the 1980s than by imprudent acts by the Third World making huge efforts simply to survive.

What if the Amazon region is burning? Let us recall the words of Luiz Inacio da Silva (leader of the Brazilian Workers' Party, and universally known as 'Lula')[6] at the funeral of Chico Mendes: 'If the Amazon is the lungs of the

Earth, debt is the pneumonia.' Let us recall, above all, that despite all the burning that goes on, Brazil, with three times the population of France, produces 20 per cent less greenhouse gases. Rather than the Amazon region, let us remember our factories and our motor cars. We will certainly need, in the next ten years, an international treaty to fix quotas concerning the right of each national community to pillage and pollute the various components of the biosphere. The Climate Convention signed in Rio in 1992 lays down principles giving 'developed' countries no greater rights, relative to their population, than countries of the Third World. For developed countries, quotas will be much more constraining. For them, it is the whole of their development model, the whole of their social compromises established at nature's expense, which will have to be re-examined downwards.

Similarly, social clauses on free trade will stop them continuing to pillage the labour and natural resources of the Third World. No majority in the North will agree to this without a change *in the North* of the ideal of progress. More free time and community services, the return to a more convivial and less predatory concept of the joy of life, will need to replace productivism and the worship of consumption. In short, changing oneself is the best way of helping others.

If the ecologist alternative to the old Left does not take on board these objectives, it is nonsense to speak of help for the Third World. To quote the conclusion to the summit conference of seven of the poorest countries in Paris in July 1989, held at the same time as the Big Seven summit:

A radical revision of the development model imposed by the North on the South is essential, in the interests of the North and not just the South. Every development model must:

respect human dignity, political freedoms, the environment, the identity, values and basic needs of peoples; guarantee women the same economic and social opportunities as men; lead to an equitable distribution of resources and decision-making power in all areas.

8

The North–South Divide: Reality or Outmoded Concept?

In what I have said up to now, I may well have provoked a certain scepticism concerning the North–South divide: it may be argued that the notions of North and South are rather outdated, with new industrial powers emerging in the South, and ghettos and poverty riots in Great Britain, the old imperial power, and in the United States, its successor.

Such a statement is, at least in retrospect, self-evident, yet it needs to be looked at carefully. The South has never been a homogeneous reality, even less so than the North (the most developed capitalist countries). Nevertheless, the dividing-line between North and South is as old as the expansion of market capitalism, but with varying constituents; and the South is the 'wrong' side of the North–South line, defined politically and economically. The South is the side where capitalism is not developed, or 'less well' developed – according to its own criteria – than the North. The line is drawn in terms of geography, but there are in the South dominant social groups who live as well as in the North, and in the North oppressed groups almost as disadvantaged as in the South, but it remains true that, even with all its rich people, the South is still the South, and, with all its poor people, the North is still the North. Therefore, although the different parts of the South are not defined only in terms of their relationship with the North (in this sense the 'North–South' metaphor is less reductive than the 'centre–periphery' metaphor), there has indeed been, in our common history, a single South defined in terms of its relationship with the North. But this has not always been the same one, and the distinction does not have the same relevance for all countries in the South. In this way, the 'North–South divide' may sometimes seem outmoded. My own view is rather that, until there is a new order, what is happening is that there are changes in the *nature* of the divide – changes which sometimes coincide with shifts in geographical divide. Finland is (dare I say?) no longer part of the 'South'; Argentina and the former Soviet Union have thought they would be no longer part; Korea is in the process of leaving; Portugal has become part of it, but is trying to leave again.

The ambiguities of decolonization

The great European expansion, of which 1992 saw the 500th anniversary, divided North and South and created the two opposing groups of colonizers and colonized. The same division operated in the other direction (decolonization) from the end of the eighteenth century. However, differences between the two were immediately apparent: whereas world conquest by countries of north-west Europe continued, decolonization in the American continent gave rise, not to societies ruled by native peoples, but to Creole states. The main example of this, the United States of America, quickly lined up with the North, massacring natives in the west and pushing back other Creoles (Mexicans) in the south. When Latin America became independent, one thing was obvious – political independence was not enough to become part of the 'North'. At the same time, moreover, the home countries of the Turkish, Spanish and Portuguese empires became part of the South – the *new* South based on a new economic division of the world.[1]

This ambiguity – countries which were politically independent but economically dependent – took a long time to resolve. Throughout the nineteenth century, in the name of politico-economic liberalism, the United States managed to appear as 'liberator of the South' (that is, of colonies) while at the same time pursuing the economic penetration of Creole or native societies. This ruse, backed by the Monroe Doctrine, held out until the Mexican Revolution, failed in the case of Commodore Perry's expedition to Japan, but again succeeded unobtrusively in the Boxer Wars against China, in alliance with Europe and Japan.

In this 'classic' period of colonialism, the situation is reasonably clear despite the hypocrisy of official pronouncements. Whether through colonization or liberal decolonization, there was established, fairly consciously on the part of the North, a first *international division of labour* which the British economist David Ricardo had described and analysed at the beginning of the nineteenth century. In the South were markets for manufactured goods, and sources of raw materials which *by chance* were not available in the North, or which were cheaper to produce in the South for ecological and social reasons. The North had coal, but its sugar, wheat and meat were too expensive, and there was no coffee . . .

The division of labour was therefore mainly about the 'conquest of markets', but it also involved the pillage of resources. Reactions in the South were varied: the Meiji empire resisted, the native peoples of Madagascar were smashed, but most of the time there were local oligarchies which chose, on behalf of their nation, to participate in this North–South relationship, not as yet widely challenged. These oligarchies bought magnificent products from the North, in exchange for the resources which they surrendered to it.

The Mexican Revolution, the first major one of this century, was both anti-oligarchic in domestic terms and nationalist in foreign policy; it was a Creole and mixed-race revolution, but with some support from native peoples, in a country which had long been decolonized. It opened a new period which lasted until after the Second World War, with the last great war of decolonization, the War of Algerian Independence (which the United States again allowed itself to support). It was the period when the North–South divide moved explicitly towards an essentially economic form of the first international division of labour.

In this extremely volatile period, the locus of the dramatic and tragic heart of the twentieth century, three movements existed at the same time:

1 The beginning of the end of political decolonization, hastened by Japan's defeat of the European empires during the Second World War, with the magnificent but harrowing masterstroke of Indian independence.
2 The rise of strategies for economic independence, brought about by anti-oligarchic revolutions and implemented by industrialization through import substitution, under populist governments which were usually Creole, but with

support from mixed-race workers and peasants: Cardenas in Mexico, Vargas in Brazil, Peron in Argentina.

3 The birth, rise and triumph of 'real socialism', a project for breaking out from colonial or 'neo-colonial' relations through an anti-capitalist revolution.

The stroke of genius of the heirs of the October Revolution in Russia (one of the 'independent-dependent' countries of the previous period) was in offering these disparate causes a theory to justify their community of interest against imperialism. A brief analysis would be: the initial international division of labour was an economic necessity for capitalism in the North. Therefore all revolutions for political independence in the South would encounter this obstacle to their economic development. The bourgeoisie in the various countries (who were opposed to oligarchies which 'bought into' the first international division of labour) were therefore objective allies of their own peoples against the imperialist North. They could be allowed a certain time for their illusion (or the responsibility for a national bourgeois democratic revolution), but very quickly the underclasses moved to the next (socialist) stage, given the failure of 'national' capitalist development – which was not necessarily Creole any more, in that the new wave of decolonization in Africa and Asia brought to power native but Westernized bourgeoisies.

The Chinese Revolution of 1949 was the culmination of this strategy. At the same time, however, Latin America launched into more or less successful national-populist revolutions which were not at all communist. At the end of the Second World War, Argentina had the fifth highest wage levels in the world; it and the Soviet Union seemed to be about to cross the dividing-line from South to North, though by different routes. These routes, however, were different in appearance only – the grand alliance against the North-West, not really altered by the emergence at the Bandung Conference of the Non-Aligned Movement (a Third World neither imperialist nor necessarily communist but allied to the 'socialist camp'), was not a simple concept dreamed up by Soviet diplomacy. In fact, social blocs which were more or less identical (alliance of a 'developmentalist' ruling class and a workers' aristocracy within a single party) were in both cases applying industrial strategies which were very close – import substitution, starting with either light industries or (more expensive and risky) heavy industries. In any case, the aim was to catch up with the Western industrial model – whether native or not, the South is culturally Creole, and makes no allowance for native or peasant interests, their culture or standard of living.

This similarity and this Achilles' heel survived during the period 1962–73, the classical age of 'anti-neocolonialism'; a period when North–South confrontation and its theorization apparently matched.

During the 1960s, however, the USSR seemed to move over to the North, after the split in the international communist movement induced by China, which asserted the need for a different model more favourable to peasant masses. The alliance between orthodox communists and developmentalists was broken in a bloodbath, from Indonesia to Brazil. Nevertheless, Suharto, the Brazilian generals and the Popular Unity Movement in Chile all dreamed of a model which would allow them to catch up through import substitution, which the United Nations Economic Commission for Latin America had theorized about since the previous period. The argument was the same as before:

'developmentalists' thought they could catch up the North through capitalism, while Marxists-turned-'dependentists' were convinced they could never catch up, since the North would never allow competitors to emerge. History seemed to come down on the side of the latter: the failure of Allende, after that of Peronism and Goulart in Brazil, marked the end of this strategy in 1973. However, the analysis of this failure by dependentists was by and large wrong.

In fact, the North no longer needed the South as an 'outlet', since it had found this in its own domestic markets, with the introduction of a model of mass production for mass consumption (Fordism). The North no longer needed the South except in the other direction – as supplier of low-cost raw materials. We have reached the classical situation, not of forced sales to the Third World (as in the time of Perry), but of 'the pillage of the Third World'.

The break-up of the Third World

This is the Achilles' heel of the strategy of industrialization through import substitution. Countries in the South need to equip with machinery from the North. Therefore they need to stay within the confines of the 'old' division of labour, and acquire foreign currency by forging ahead with traditional exports. Therefore they cannot raise the standard of living of the peasants and miners producing these raw material exports. Therefore they cannot expand their domestic market. Therefore their new industries cannot mass-produce as competitively as the North. Therefore these industries cannot pay (by exporting manufactures) for imports of capital goods. Therefore countries in the South have to go on exporting raw materials. And we have come full circle.

A by-product of this unfortunate situation was that, whether they tried industrialization like Brazil, or stuck to their old speciality like Colombia, all countries in the South depended on world prices for raw materials, to buy either consumer goods as before or capital goods. The North–South divide was a matter of balance of payments and export prices. It was therefore also the classical age of debate on 'terms of trade' and 'repatriation of profits by predatory multinationals'.

Agreement in the South on simple objectives broke down completely therefore in 1973; there was the fall of Allende (because copper prices were too low?), but also the turn-round in terms of trade for oil-exporting countries, which soon became major financial powers. There were also, in the main unnoticed, the first successes of the 'newly industrializing countries' (NICs).

For a few miraculous years, the South thought it had found the way round the obstacle, through the cartelization of exports, based on the example of oil. However, this dream of a new international economic order on the part of the United Nations Conference on Trade and Development (UNCTAD) and the South's 'Group of 77', supported by China in the diplomatic arena, this brief period of political unity against the North, in fact hid a new break-up of the South. There were countries stuck with the old international division of labour, for the better (OPEC), or for the worse (Africa). There were others bogged down in the failure of import substitution, or hoping to relaunch the process using the windfall of oil (Mexico, Iran). And there were the NICs.

This was industrialization in order to export, taking advantage of low wage levels. The economic situation was just right, with the North running out of steam but still a huge open market. The pool of petrodollars was flooding the world with easy credit. Brazil took advantage of it to play all its cards at once – import substitution and export-led industrialization. A *new international division of labour* was superimposed on the previous one: the North exports (on credit) sophisticated capital goods, the South pays for them with manufactured goods, but ordinary unsophisticated ones.

The foundations of *technological dependence* were laid; but this was overtaken at the end of the 1970s by the *monetarist shock* which inaugurated, for the following ten years, the theme of *financial dependence*. Unilaterally, the North (in reality, the United States Federal Reserve) reversed the terms of credit by a huge rise in interest rates, while organizing a recession in its own economies. The debt service burden became overwhelming, and markets for the South's industries narrowed.

In the nightmare scenario, a financial Hiroshima struck Latin America, Africa and Asia.[2] Only the 'dragons', the NICs of East Asia, which had secured their loans on powerful export-oriented industries, withstood the shock. When the United States in its turn in 1983 embarked on a credit-based expansion, the NICs of Asia took advantage of this huge market to export themselves out of debt. However, Brazil, despite a dramatic fall in imports and a tremendous export effort (a $15 billion surplus in 1990, $30 billion in 1991), did not manage to pay back its debts.

By the beginning of the 1990s, the South was exhausted, politically on its knees and certainly fragmented. Even indebtedness had not managed to bring about a 'Southern front' – this was tried in vain, at least as far as Latin America was concerned, at Cartagena. Nevertheless, the South had a weapon at its disposal which was a powerful deterrent for the North – co-ordinated non-repayment of debt. Using this weapon in an unplanned, individualist way, the South managed to extract partial moratoria and reductions. What Susan George has called 'the boomerang effect'[3] of the South's dire situation also threatened the North: severe competition for low-price exports; pillage of the 'common heritage of humanity' (forests, atmosphere) in order to survive by exporting, by literally feeding the flames; export of narcotic drugs; rampant nationalist and fundamentalist movements.

However, the guiding principle was still 'divide and rule'. The second Gulf War allowed the North to liquidate its powerful mercenary Iraq, which it had armed to fight Iran in the first Gulf War; moreover, new help became available from the rich 'petromonarchies', plus Syria and particularly Egypt, which were rewarded with a timely reduction of their crippling debts.

The strength of the poor

By 1991, therefore, the South, now joined by former communist countries whose industry was devastated by the ill-thought-out move to a market economy, offered a sorry spectacle to the now-forgotten 1960s prophets of economic independence. Having burned their fingers by industrializing on money market loans, countries in the South begged the multinationals to return with their direct investment – even though this would be financed by debt–equity swaps. Under pressure to export, they became the proponents of free trade at a time when the protectionist North barricaded itself against the great price-cutting flood.

The year 1991, however, was when the South became aware that, despite its tremendous weakness, it still had the one strength which the poor have – a nuisance value. The productivist-export distortion of its development models, forced on it by the debt crisis, began to increase considerably the part played by the South in the planet's rate of ecological destabilization. The North, directly responsible for most of this degradation, and indirectly responsible (by its own example and by debt pressures) for unsustainable development models foisted on the South, launched a world-scale negotiation. Very quickly the South, under the leadership of China and India, with Malaysia playing the role of 'the Saddam Hussein of the environment', saw the chance to work a deal: 'OK, we do want to do something about the environment. But we want development. Meet the extra costs of sustainable development. Reduce our debts. Open your markets to our exports.'

This is the stage we have now reached. Governments in the South, whether Creole or Westernized (or Japanized?) native ones, are now threatening the North that they will follow its nineteenth-century model. However, the historical irony is that native peoples, from the Chipko movement in India to the Indians of Amazonia, are now also saying in NGO circles, 'Yes, sustainable development is possible, but it will be very different from the one in the North.'

Once more surprisingly reunited against the North–South divide, the South is still just as diverse in its aspirations as in its living conditions. The Western development model has not totally failed in the South (it works extremely well in East

Asia), but any future success is a threat to the planet, in the South as well as the North.

Will humanity invent a model of sustainable development involving solidarity of North and South? Or will the North–South divide take the form of a war of the environment? This is the big issue of the twenty-first century.[4]

9

The Rio Conference and New North–South Relations

The second United Nations Conference on Environment and Development in June 1992 in Rio de Janeiro will be seen as a decisive step towards consciousness that humankind is united in facing the catastrophe which its madness has brought to the planet. For ages, ecologists have been actively campaigning for thinking on a global scale, for a leap forward in the sense of responsibility, for a globally concerted fight against unsustainable models of development; we can congratulate ourselves wholeheartedly on the emergence of the desire for an agreement on the world ecological order.

It has to be said, however, that the Rio Conference started off badly, in that it came just after a change in the locus of world tension. Just as East–West rivalry disappeared, the real confrontation – between North and South – became fully apparent. With the Gulf War, the North cynically proclaimed its conception of the new world order: the law of double standards, the mote and the beam, the lion and the donkey.

Barricaded behind frontiers closed to refugees fleeing disasters which it provoked, the North, and in particular the

United States, felt it could impose its choices and its 'justice' on the South through cruise missiles, frozen loan accounts, IMF reconstruction plans and food blockades. It set up a new 'wall of shame' between the rich and the 'barbarians', between the United States and Mexico – a wall at the heart of Europe, between Italy and Albania, between Slovenia and Kosovo, between Hungary and Romania; a wall round the richest nations of Europe, gradually abandoning to unemployment and the Mafia the Mediterranean islands, and soon the south of Italy . . .[1]

The trap

All this means that concern for the environment can be shamelessly used against the South's development needs by those very states which for a century and a half enslaved the world and ravaged the planet. It is quite simple: if the South goes on developing, its contribution to the greenhouse effect will soon be greater than the North's. If it continues to chop down forests and industrialize its agriculture, biodiversity will disappear from the planet. To save these 'common possessions of humanity' without jeopardizing Northern models, we simply prevent the South from imitating the North. The Rio Conference was in danger of becoming a confrontation between the replete productivisms of the North and the ambitious productivisms of dictatorships in the South; the losers would be a great flood of Third World peasants and poor people of shanty towns, for whom the only sustainable development is the protection and rehabilitation of their environment.

In reality, we must reject this false dilemma. There is no contradiction between environment and development; development for the vast majority of the planet is above all the right to health, the right to a life free from the struggle to survive. This struggle is crippling for the earth, for the forests, for human beings and above all for women. *There is no sustainable development for nature but one which is based on solidarity between human beings.*

The biggest trap facing ecologists and 'Third-Worldists', in both North and South, in the run-up to Rio was the alleged contradiction between development and environment. Lack of consciousness on the one hand, and Machiavellism on the other sprang this trap. The trap nearly worked, and it may still work! NGOs, as advanced expressions of an emerging world public opinion, are in the best position to prevent the jaws of the trap closing on its victim.

The first 'jaw' is the selfishness of the North, the distorted vision which makes it denounce the burning mote in the fields of the South and ignore the beam in its own furnaces, its contempt for the 'fast-breeding' populations of the South, its hypocrisy in defending wild animals in African reserves while wiping out Indians in reserves set up by itself. A case of naturalism pitted against humanism, environment against development. The second 'jaw' of the trap is the cynicism and short-sightedness of ruling classes in the South – power-crazed generals and advocates of unrestrained capitalism. As a Malaysian Prime Minister said, 'Ecology, worker protection, democracy, human rights – these are simply obstacles erected by the North to stop the development of its future competitors.' Development (and what development!) pitted against ecology . . .

As NGOs in the development and environment field are perfectly aware, the contradiction between the two is limited to a few specific cases, which need to be looked at and accounted for. It may not be only in Rwanda and Burundi that local people's maize fields end in barbed wire fences protecting natural reserves; but for the vast majority of the planet, for poor peasants and shanty-town masses, development is first and foremost improvement of the environment. Men and women of Africa and South Asia will stop exhausting themselves, while exhausting nature, by learning more efficient techniques of food preparation, moving to less rapacious kinds of farming, and cleaning up their water supply. Car users in the North will best help cyclone-hit Bangladesh by stopping the global warming brought about by burning fossil fuels.

Who exactly are the people operating the jaws of the trap? The 'jaw' of 'environment without development' is made up of elites in the North who want to keep the Amazon Basin as a free holding-ground for genetic diversity, as an air-conditioning plant, as a thermostat of their own madness. The other 'jaw' of 'development without environment' consists of the middle classes in 'middle' countries, and of rich people in those poor countries which aspire to the wastage levels of the 'really rich', by riding roughshod over the material well-being of their own population, by ravaging the ecosystem of their own country, and by despoiling the heritage of their own children.

Nevertheless, a year before the Rio Conference, all over the world and particularly in France, NGOs in the development and environment field were at each other's throats, as if they were obliged to line up on one side or the other. Was it a case of suspicions, groups not used to working together, inferiority complex on the part of 'young and penniless' French environment NGOs when faced with 'big' development NGOs? Was it inhibitions on the part of 'poor' development NGOs in Latin countries concerning 'rich' environment NGOs in the English-speaking world? No doubt these were relevant, but the environment/development split was an important factor, albeit in milder forms. One of these is 'ecological radicalism', based on rejection of any technological progress which does not involve challenging certain aspects of the dominant development model (for example, the Goldemberg scenario of energy saving is condemned as 'ecoproductivism' by intellectuals in the North who have no hesitation in flying out to visit their neolithic tribes in the South).[2] At the other end of the spectrum is a kind of terrorist humanism which, in defending the poor of today, even against environmental conservation, totally ignores the interests of the poor of tomorrow.

All these contradictions are real ones. Life is full of them. The complexity of the world cannot be reduced to some 'overriding issue'. When subjectively we pit one thing against another, we have to regard these cases as real problems, to be solved by working together, in the North and in the South, and by the North working with the South. This long journey was embarked on, far removed from the eyes of the world's press, in the run-up to the Rio Conference.

About-turn at the Earth Summit

What happened at Rio, in the final stage of negotiations, would have been totally unthinkable barely a year earlier. Above and beyond the twists and turns of the American delegation and the humiliations heaped by the State Department on delegation head William Reilly (the United States

Environment Secretary), we witnessed a significant diplomatic event: the United States lost the first battle in the war of the environment which they themselves had started.

Let us be totally clear about what was at stake in this war. Press commentators who scoffed at the meagre achievements of the Earth Summit by saying, 'Once again, the mountain has given birth to a mouse', seem to be unaware of the magnitude of the global ecological crisis about to happen in the first half of the twenty-first century. The only meaningful comparison is when half the population of Europe was wiped out in the fourteenth century. This needed two centuries of recovery and a total change in agricultural techniques and land-tenure law: a move to polyculture and co-operative animal breeding, the removal of seigneurial rights and the enclosure of common land: not the kind of thing to be put right in two years of negotiating, but developments involving wars and revolutions. All that Rio could do was underline the urgency of local and global threats (which was at least one major achievement); all that could be expected at Rio was an affirmation of overriding principles; all that could be done was to open up the debate on the fundamental question: 'Who should take on the bulk of the effort?' It was on this aspect that there was a totally unexpected outcome.

Two years before the conference, the roles seemed to have been assigned. 'Rio' was going to be about forests. Biodiversity was going to be about forests. What of the greenhouse effect? Once again, forests. Forests which are being burnt down by mad dictators in the Third World, by productivist elites in the South, by ignorant peasant masses. Armed with their conscience and their right to rule the world, buttressed by their 'crusade of righteousness' in the Gulf War, governments in the North, with the United States at their head and supported by their bright-eyed NGOs, were going to spread the good word and smash the Saddam Husseins of the environment – the governors of the Amazon Basin, the Prime Minister of Malaysia . . .

In Rio, however, the United States was branded as the bad guy of history. The Saddam Hussein of the environment was George Bush. Abandoned by their most faithful allies, Canada, the United Kingdom and France, the Americans were completely isolated, while the European Community could afford to express regret that the North had not yet done anything meaningful, and Japan was already offering the technology to apply the good resolutions yet to be made.

Rio revealed what the Gulf War had concealed: despite their unbroken military hegemony, the United States has lost its hegemony in the technological and financial, and now in the political, fields.

Already, by signing the Climate Convention in May 1992, it was conceding on three major points over which it had fought at the Geneva Climate Conference in autumn 1990. Without committing itself to a definite timetable for reducing its own emissions, it did accept the need to bring greenhouse gas emissions down to 1990 levels by the year 2000. Moreover, this reduction would first cover specifically carbon dioxide and not an overall blanket reduction of both carbon gases from cars in the North and methane from rice-fields in the South. A final point was that the reduction would apply initially only to the North, with the South having the right to increase its share of the atmospheric cake.

On biodiversity, however, North American industrial interests resisted, and refused to take the medicine; their position was that 'molecules in forests and traditional peasants' fields are free, those from laboratories are not.' Countries in the South and NGOs imposed a fairer share-out of rights: the Biodiversity Convention recognized countries' rights to their natural biological wealth and implied that discoveries from genetic research should be in the public domain. The United States did not sign this convention. It was the only country not to sign, but it could not hold out for ever, and later the Clinton administration agreed to sign.

This spectacular turnaround was no doubt partly due to the presumptuousness of a Bush administration drunk on the success of its bombers in the Iraqi desert; but the main reason was the tremendous mobilization of NGOs in the third and fourth preparatory committees of the Earth Summit, and in the Ya Wananchi conference of NGOs in Paris in December 1991. It was particularly NGOs from the South which jolted the conscience of the North and the timidity of their own governments, managed to rally powerful environmentalist NGOs in the North (Greenpeace, Friends of the Earth, World Wildlife Fund), and overturned stereotypes such as 'waste is caused by the South' and 'ecology is the luxury of the rich'.

Is ecology in fact a luxury of rich countries? How could we have forgotten that, in the nineteenth century, the first or-ganized workers' struggles in the countries of the Industrial Revolution were first and foremost struggles for the ecology of work, the reduction in working hours from fourteen hours a day to ten, then to eight, the abolition of child labour, the regulation of dangerous and dirty jobs? How could we have forgotten that 'bourgeois socialism', consisting of unilateral moves by 'philanthropic' capitalists to protect 'their' work-ers, was often called *hygienism* – the fight against slums and tuberculosis? Frantic mass consumption by the North's wage-earning class is only half a century old, and postdated victories in the campaigns for a healthy working environment and the right to decent housing. Moreover, popular common sense has always put health before material riches.

In countries of the South, where work and quality of life are even more closely related to 'the environment', popular ecology (this time authentically a 'deep ecology') had not lost sight of the relative importance of these imperatives: 'the worst pollution is poverty.' This slogan was no doubt one-sided (since opulence is just as dangerous), but it received a drubbing in Rio.

What was defeated in Rio was a view of ecological order as a means of blackmailing and control by wasteful countries over dominated countries. This view, inspired by the Bush administration (and not by the 'deep ecology' attacked by those whose knowledge of ecology comes from books), was defeated, but at a heavy price. Faced with the diplomatic pressure of those who 'blamed the victims', we saw grass-roots organizations from Malaysia side with their own government, which in reality tries to repress them when they fight against the destruction of forests. We saw Latin American feminists, who in their own countries fight for abortion and contraception as a woman's right to her own body, indignantly reject the strictures of immodest internationalism (delivered by people such as Commander Cousteau), which denounced rising birth rates (in the South!) as a threat to global ecology, when in fact each child in Niger consumes 250 times less than a child in the United States . . .

The real questions have finally been asked. Will the North question its own development model? Will it help the South implement sustainable development? These are the issues for future battles by NGOs and ecologist movements against irresponsible productivist elites in the North . . . but also in the South.

What now?

Of course we must regulate access to the common heritage of humanity – the ability of the terrestrial ecosystem to resist the distortions of the greenhouse effect, to maintain its biological diversity and so on. Of course we must limit the right to atmospheric emission of dangerous gases (carbon gases, methane, CFCs). But this cannot be done by fixing ceilings or percentage reductions, since this would give rich countries, the prime polluters, an infinitely bigger right to pollute than other countries. The right of access to the common heritage must be shared between countries in proportion to their population; this is what countries in the South are demanding, to ensure the right of their people to decent living conditions.

This means that the North must abandon its shamefully wasteful practices. Priority use of the planet's atmosphere must be given to the food-producing South and not the car-using North. Clearly, this world-scale 'night of 4 August' (when the French nobility surrendered its privileges in 1789), this surrender by the North of privileges which are leading the Earth to catastrophe, could not take place at Rio. What began was a prolonged cultural revolution. What is at stake is our common destiny.

It is not enough, however, to give the South rights which it is technologically and financially unable to exercise. Huge transfers of technology and finance are needed to give the South access to sustainable development. First and foremost is the need to abolish the debt burden which crushes the people of the South and leads them to seek survival in productive practices which nature cannot sustain. Even transfers of this kind will not be enough if the peoples of the South remain under the yoke of dictatorships, which the North sustains as long as they serve its interests, then crushes with bombs when they assert themselves, and if they remain under laws which deny women the right to their own bodies.

Aid and financial transfers should be given first to popular non-governmental associations, to popular movements fighting for human emancipation, on the basis of respect for the natural environment. Financial pressure and trade embargoes are justified against dictatorships, provided such measures are taken in co-ordination with democratic and ecologist opposition groups.

All this depends on the emergence of a world-scale public opinion concerned with solidarity and justice, responsible with regard to future generations and life on the planet. The responsibility for promoting this public opinion lies pre-eminently with world Green movements. Europe has a key role to play in this front against the World War of the environment, in this fight for a peaceful world based on solidarity.[3] Europe has the financial and technological resources; it is in Europe that the ecological movement is working hardest on public opinion and is beginning to break through to institutions. Europe is a microcosm of the world in the income and development differentials between its countries, and in its unification process is experimenting with new transnational modes of regulation.

Experimenting inevitably means making mistakes. The Maastricht agreement was one of these mistakes, which history will have to learn to put right, and start again. The next two chapters will analyse this mistake.

10

Pro-Europe Means Anti-Maastricht

Referenda and parliamentary votes on the Maastricht Treaty have to be clearly seen for what they were: not votes about European unification, but about a *proposed* constitution for a political Europe, a constitution establishing the ground rules – what could be decided or not decided, and who could do the deciding – and for some time to come, since a constitution cannot be changed like an article of clothing. Ecologists, who support European political union as a step towards a better-ordered world, had to pronounce on this particular constitution, and not on the idea of a political Europe. In the same way, the French 1958 referendum on the constitution of the Fifth Republic was not a vote for or against France, nor about a Republic as such.

A constitution does not establish the details of laws and social compromises, though clearly it is never neutral on such matters. A constitution establishes the relative importance of the various actors, and a list of what is allowed and not allowed, implying where matters can develop and where there will be blockages. In evaluating these ground rules, ecologists ask whether they favour a move to a Europe with greater ecological responsibility and more social solidarity, greater control of public authorities by citizens, and more solidarity with countries poorer than itself.

The Maastricht Treaty, even more powerful in legal terms than a constitution, is at least clear on all these points, in that it goes further than formal procedures. It is explicit on the social philosophy it wants to achieve, it establishes rules and basic guidelines which in the normal course of things would be developed later in laws and policies. It goes beyond the usual rules of procedure by establishing end results and the means to achieve them.

The end result is to be 'a market economy under free competition' – not in the sense of the existence of a market, but in the sense of rolling back everything not subject to the market – everything whereby democracies since 1945 had managed to reduce the excesses of blind market forces. For example, it is expressly stated that central banks cannot finance public deficits, and that preferential loans cannot be made to public undertakings or organizations (such as social housing agencies).

A monetarist hard core

The most significant part of this ultra-liberal, and literally *monetarist*, option is the decision to go for a single currency, issued by a central bank *outside democratic control*, as central banks were before the 1930s depression. The model is already there in the German Bundesbank, which, in opposition to all European governments, *including that of Chancellor Kohl*, pursued a dear-money policy which ruined the possibility of the smooth incorporation of East Germany and heightened economic and social tensions throughout Europe.

Now that politicians have given up ascribing all virtue to economic and monetary union, and since the financial markets have destroyed any possibility of achieving it, we must, in order to start off on a new footing, try to understand:

1 why a major Nobel prize-winning economist, Paul Samuelson, said that a 'yes' vote in the French referendum on Maastricht would have no significance, since this is not how a currency is introduced;
2 why Ralf Dahrendorf, a former EEC Commissioner (1970–4), could say that the racist disturbances in Rostock were 'Europe's fault' and condemn Maastricht;[1]
3 why Michel Rocard, who in campaigning in favour of the treaty delivered scathing attacks on its opponents, later said that 'an independent central bank is dogma bordering on stupidity' and recognized that 'over the next thirty years, it will cause us dramatic crises'.[2]

The projected economic and monetary union rests on three major elements:

1   creating an independent central bank;
2   to move by forced marches;
3   towards a single currency.

These three elements are all derived from the same monetarist dogma – the idea that the amount of money in circulation is determined by experts, and that its flow is the sole influence on inflation rates. However, currency is more than that – it is a social linkage, an institution which crystallizes social compromises; on the rate of money supply depend not just inflation (which itself depends on a host of other social factors),[3] but also employment, investment and exchange rates. It follows that restricting money supply by a high interest rate policy amounts to ruining the real economy simply to bring the 'economic temperature' (the inflation rate) down a few degrees.

The autumn 1992 and July 1993 crises in the European Monetary System were a reminder of something which is self-evident: rates of inflation in Europe are different for objective reasons. Freezing parities before ironing out these differences can only lead to adjustment problems. A *common* European currency may be desirable in addition to local (national) ones, not to facilitate travel or (a dafter argument) to allow intra-European financial transfers, but for the advantages to be gained from issuing credible means of payment; moreover, it could be established straight away. However, one cannot create a *single* currency for all countries until their inflation rates converge, which involves co-ordinating social compromises.

The Maastricht Treaty tries to solve the problem by the crude method of 'convergence criteria' involving a system of sanctions. This would mean, for southern Europe, adjustment plans comparable to those which the IMF imposes on Latin America. It is the application of plans of this kind which caused the crisis in Italy, with a split between North and South, between workers and trade union leaders, and so on. The threat of a 'Rostockization' of Italy, together with a splitting-off of Lombardy, like Slovenia from Yugoslavia, has been created by Maastricht *as a process*.

Moreover, what is also problematical is *the aim* itself of Maastricht: a central bank, running monetary policy with complete independence, while the European Council (European Union summit meetings) would manage the rest of economic policy. This split is absurd – fixing interest rates at a particular level would be bound to affect unemployment rates more than inflation rates. More unacceptable, however, is the lack of political accountability of a small band of high financiers. The argument is that this would allow all countries, and not just Germany, to participate in managing the single currency. There we are: Monsieur La Génière, Monsieur de Larosière, or others, will represent in a central bank the interests of European peoples, just as they have represented them in the IMF . . .

West Germany enjoyed the advantages of an independent central bank for as long as the interests of the bank, industry and trade unions coincided. This was no longer so after reunification – the Bundesbank became the major obstacle to the trouble-free integration of both parts of Germany.

Europe can only be built with the consensus of its peoples. The attempt to unify it through the straitjacket of monetarism is turning them against Europe. Sacrificing jobs, nature and even the productive system on the altar of an independent currency is a return to the concept of money prevalent before the Great Depression of the 1930s, before the 'Great Transformation' of the 1940s and before the social compromises of the Liberation.[4] In other words, the very foundations of social compromises of the social democratic type are jeopardized. One may not like social democracy, but what is surprising is a constitution which rules out future social democratic laws and policies, not to speak of ecologist policies.

An anti-ecology and anti-social Europe

Apart from the explicit monetarist proposals, what must be looked at are the *implicit* consequences of the mechanisms established by Maastricht. Here what is permitted by the treaty (tacitly as well as overtly) is just as important as what is forbidden.

The ecological consequences of what is implied became immediately obvious to the European Community's 'Minister of the Environment', Carlo Ripa de Meana, who condemned Maastricht as a 'trick'.[5] Everything to do with sustainable development is in fact governed in the treaty by the unanimity rule among governments. It only needs one or two countries to play the 'ecological dumping' card (that is, relax their own regulations to attract industries which pollute) for them to block all progress in a particular area, even if the European Parliament and most countries are in favour. Moreover, since countries are not allowed to protect themselves against another country's ecological dumping, the end result is clear: no country, unless it is very competitive, can risk moving forward on its own.

The example of a carbon tax to counter the greenhouse effect is pertinent. I referred in my book *Berlin, Baghdad, Rio*[6] to the central role which this carbon tax was destined to play in efforts by the European Commission, and the French government, to take the world lead at Rio in environment matters. As soon as Maastricht was signed, Ripa de Meana was predicting that 'we will be going to Rio with empty hands'; and in fact industrial interests lobbied against the carbon tax throughout the first half of 1992, arguing that it threatened high-energy-consuming sectors. They were supported, as expected, by the British and Spanish governments. The project foundered, and allowed the French government, which was only lukewarm, to hide behind the rejection by the other two countries. Everybody then hid behind rejection by the United States, and in May 1992 the European summit said there would be no EEC carbon tax so long as it was not adopted throughout the industrialized world! It would, however, have been quite feasible, in the context of Rio, to put a European carbon tax element on to all goods imported into Europe.

The same thing happened on the social front: already the Single Act, by establishing the free movement of goods and capital without unifying the social context of competition, had invited firms to locate where the workforce could be best exploited, thus giving them the means of blackmailing employees in high-wage countries.

Monetary union, without tax harmonization, further strengthens the hand of the owners of capital, a point emphasized, not without cynicism, by economists supporting Maastricht.[7] The argument runs:

1 Loss of monetary autonomy by countries leaves only fiscal policy to boost the competitiveness of their firms . . . by reducing their taxes.
2 Since 'cultural obstacles to mobility of labour' discourage movement between countries, wage earners can be taxed without fear of their emigrating to tax paradises.
3 Result: the treaty offers the possibility of a massive shift of tax advantages to the detriment of employees.

Maastricht therefore continues the approach of the Single Act by favouring monetarist Robin Hoods in reverse, taking from the poor to give to the rich.

Democracy forced to retreat

The argument will be made out that democracy is preserved, that through elections we can stop governments adopting this approach. Maastricht dealt with this aspect: it established the relationship between executives and legislatures by strengthening the spontaneous (and widespread) trend towards the autonomy of executives and bureaucracies in relation to elected parliaments. In fact, the Maastricht Treaty process was a precursor of what the Europe of Maastricht will be: the Treaty was negotiated between national executives and the Brussels technostructure. Then each government went to its people or parliament and said in effect 'take it or leave it; but if you leave it, it's the end of Europe.' The derisory 'right of co-decision' given to the European Parliament (the only supranational body elected by the citizens of Europe) is merely a polite way of denying it what history denied troublesome intruders for centuries: parliamentary rights such as the right to propose and to amend legislation. It is no doubt true that history will continue, and one day the European Parliament will 'chance its arm', as so many of its predecessors did; but in the Maastricht Treaty we were voting for a constitution, not a future *coup d'état* by the people.

As for relations with the rest of the world, once again the treaty is explicit. It does not leave common foreign and security policy to the chance of future democratic choice. The policy is fixed in advance, in the context of confrontation between North and South (now including the East) which since the Gulf War, and even in Rio, marks out the run-up to the next century. The secular arm of the European Union will be a Western European Union integrated into NATO. Other institutional structures such as the Conference on Security and Co-operation in Europe could have been given a prominent role, but this will no longer be possible . . . unless the Treaty is broken; but all in good time!

Now that the Maastricht Treaty has come into force, despite the original Danish rejection, bare acceptance by the French and reservations on the part of Britain, Europe is a technostructure on autopilot, unaffected by political changes in a particular country, favourable to capital and productivism, allied to the United States against the rest of the world. All available economic models predicted an initial four years of economic difficulties and 'structural adjustments' of a Latin American kind for southern European countries.[8] We can expect serious social tensions adding to support for separatist movements, which the stronger states will repress in ways we cannot imagine. But the supporters of Maastricht were no doubt following the precept of Napoleon and Lenin: 'Try it, and see what happens . . .'

11

And Now, a Fresh Start . . .

'Nothing will be the same again!' was the unanimous cry from French political and media circles after the 'no' surge in the September 1992 referendum, which they had not bargained for three months earlier; it was a bitter satisfaction and a source of hope for the Greens, who had been criticizing the Maastricht Treaty since the previous December.

Bitter satisfaction, because they had opposed the free-market Europe of the Single Act, and were hoping that the long-promised political Europe would be an antidote to social and ecological dumping, and especially a step forward in accountability to the people. Greens were completely taken aback on reading the Maastricht Treaty: virtually no progress on social Europe, nothing on sustainable development, minimal right of 'co-decision' for members of the European Parliament, and above all a strengthening of the move to monetarism through a monetary union whose dramatic social consequences were picked up by economists and their econometric models. Unanimously, the Green group in the European Parliament rejected the treaty. In June 1992, French Greens called on the Lisbon European summit to establish a timetable to fill all the glaring gaps in the treaty, but to no avail.

At their August 1992 conference, Jacques Delors tried a final time to convince reluctant French Greens by an assurance that 'if the imbalance is not righted between economic union and the democratic deficit, the monetary aspect of the treaty will not be applied, since ordinary people will not accept it.' But it was too late: the imbalance should have been righted at the Lisbon summit. The Greens' demands had been ignored, and ordinary people had the summer of 1992 to become aware of the disastrous consequences of the treaty. Could they really count on Jacques Delors to head demonstrations of French farmers or the unemployed of Naples against the consequences of the treaty when these became apparent?

The upshot was that supporters of a democratic, ecological and social Europe, open to the South and the East, were in a dilemma – should they vote 'yes', along with those who supported a Europe which would turn ordinary working people against it; or vote 'no', along with nationalist demagogues who were exploiting for their own purposes people's hostility to Maastricht?

As convinced Europeans, the hearts of ecologists made them lean towards a 'yes' vote; but as fully participating Europeans who had immersed themselves for many years in the debates taking place in Brussels and Strasbourg, they were well aware of the consequences of Maastricht. They could not go along with those who thought the treaty (had they read it?) was about 'a Europe of ruddy cheeks and smelling of garlic', as the right-wing French ecologist politician, Brice Lalonde, put it, whereas Maastricht was about a Europe of three-piece suits for some and hollow cheeks for others, or at least a Europe of pasteurized cheese. Reason told Greens to vote 'no'.

My own position was that of those who thought the main thing was to fight against the content of Maastricht, rather than exalting the virtues of a Europe which would be different from the one established by the treaty. For Greens, Europe is merely a means towards an ecologist policy, and political ecology cannot separate the issue of the environment from social issues. Above all, we could not let nationalist populism have the monopoly of the political expression of the cry of the oppressed, and of the 'wrong' side of a France split in two. In the referendum of 20 September 1992 the Greens were on the side of the majority of small farmers, manual and white-collar workers, and working women: the 'no' side.

Greens would never accept that this 'lower half of French society' voted through ignorance. Only too aware of the consequences – because it was experiencing its first manifestations – of a policy which Greens had been able to analyse fully, this half of a split society voted in accordance with its interests and rights. Greens are proud that they helped decisively to halt the split, by working with this half of society as resources allowed, in debates and meetings, and side by side with the most critical elements in the former 'progressive camp'. And they are proud of having carried the flag of Europe in the 'no' camp.

Modernity is no longer progressive

We need to think further about this famous 'no' by the 'lower half' of French society. It was the 'no' of a majority of workers, small farmers, office workers, young people (apart from very young males), women and traditional left-wing areas of France, as against the 'yes' of managerial groups and people with a high level of education. The 'lower reaches of society', as Alain Touraine calls them, the world of people on the verge of social exclusion and unemployment, of drop-outs and people with little formal education seemed to have turned its back on Europe, on history. Ignorant and reactionary, the ordinary people, some would argue, are today rightly represented by politicians such as Le Pen, Pasqua and Georges Marchais, respectively the leading fascist, Gaullist and communist opponents of the treaty.

However, I would like to point out the weaknesses of such an analysis, having called for a 'pro-Europe no to Maastricht', together with some Greens and dissidents from the old Left. First, the sociological characterization of both 'yes' and 'no' voters applies to small deviations around the 50 per cent vote. More than 40 per cent of manual workers voted 'yes', and more than 30 per cent of intellectual professions and higher management voted 'no'. Second, both ordinary people's 'no' vote and intellectuals' 'yes' vote were the very opposite of unreasoned. Set against 'yes'-voting intellectuals who had not read the treaty (Barbara Hendricks, Umberto Eco) or those who said there was no point in reading it (Edgar Morin) on the grounds that 'the main point is the idea of Europe', was the methodical criticism of 'professional' economists (Samuelson, Allais, Dahrendorf) and the practical experience, on the part of workers and small farmers, of exactly what 'convergence' policies were.

In other words, the 'no' vote by ordinary people was a rational vote, 'in accordance with class interests'. However, it is now regarded by the intelligentsia as reactionary. In a sense, it is reactionary: a reaction against modernity, at least against a particular kind of modernity, such as is denounced by writers like Jean Chesneaux, but gloriously exemplified by people like Elisabeth Guigou or Brice Lalonde: being modern is travelling everywhere by plane and sending one's children to higher education abroad. What is certain is that the anxious reaction of ordinary people, as symbolized in Le Pen and Pasqua and Marchais, was more representative of 'no' than sophisticated criticism by the Greens and the critical Left.

Let us face the issue squarely: ordinary people have stopped being 'modern'; in any event, they are excluded from modernity as it really is. This is a decisive break with more than a century of progressivism. In the past, one did not have to ask oneself whether one had to be on the side of the 'lower orders', since they were oppressed and humiliated (probably the main motivation of left-wing Christians), or because they represented the future (the motivation of the secular Left). Marxism supplied a dialectical link between the two: the development of productive forces (modernity) socialized people and united the strengths of labour and science; the overthrow of capitalism would open the doors of the future to the emancipated masses.

We now know that history is even more tragic than we had feared: not only is the road tortuous, but the future is not necessarily bright. Productive forces tend to pillage the planet and atomize the masses. In this divorce between modernity and ethical progressivism, communism disappeared and political ecology emerged.

Progressivism needs to be reinvented. It can no longer count on the movement of history, on the development of technology or knowledge, it can no longer be content to acclaim modernity. Moreover, modernity was simply belief in the coincidence of *change* and *progress*, in the ethically progressive nature of individual emancipation from the dead weight of the past. From now on, progressivism has a duty always to be 'on the side of the poor', in the name of an ethics of solidarity, but certainly not the 'party of the poor', since social exclusion does not promise an emancipatory dialectical reversal of fortune. It has to represent a different kind of modernity, it must come down on the side of freedom to act, to innovate, to get to know and transform the world, but at the same time it must articulate the desire for autonomy in line with the criteria of solidarity and ecological responsibility. It must also reinvent Europe.

Rebuilding Europe

Nowadays, those who called for 'yes despite the deficiencies in the Maastricht Treaty' are coming to their senses. Even Michel Rocard is hitting out at economic and monetary union. Everybody is now speaking of 'democratizing Europe', 'bringing it closer to the citizens', 'developing its social aspect'. Maastricht is politically dead: the United Kingdom and Denmark reluctantly accepted ratification with reservations; this was not the only effect of the relative success of the French 'no' campaign after the first Danish rejection. The European Monetary System crises in September 1992 and July 1993 also underlined the dead-end nature of the monetary union concept at the heart of the treaty – the unreality of outdated parities which it was nevertheless intended to fix at existing levels; the unaccountability of an independent central bank (the Bundesbank) which led Europe into recession.

This 'posthumous success' of opponents of the treaty is a tremendous source of hope for them, and a heavy responsibility. The free-market approach which inspired Maastricht had already split French society, led Western Europe to the brink of division and turned the 'excluded' half of French society against Europe. It is up to pro-Europeans, those in favour of 'no, because of Maastricht' or 'yes, despite Maastricht' to start afresh.

The first task is to relaunch ecological and social Europe. Ecologists had no need of Maastricht to make France introduce catalytic converters, or Germany stop exporting nuclear waste. They are quite capable, country by country and all together, of fighting the battle against the greenhouse effect, to which Europe committed itself by its pronouncements in Rio. If they work in unison, trade unions in Europe will be able, through negotiated agreement, to impose on British employers the rules of a European social chapter from which they were absolved by Maastricht.

Necessity and pragmatism will impose the common currency which exists already, the ECU, against which each country will establish, at its own pace, a fixed parity, without going through the madness of 'rules of convergence' which are as draconian as the dire 'adjustment plans' imposed by the IMF on the Third World. Imagination and realism are needed to establish the rules of conduct of the central bank responsible for administering this common currency. The Maastricht Treaty established an absurd division of responsibilities: the central bank, acting independently, determines credit policy on the basis of the single aim of fighting inflation; the intergovernmental Council of Ministers or European summits deal with everything else. This division is absurd because credit policy is the most cumbersome of anti-inflation measures, and because it *also* has a widespread effect on unemployment, exchange rates and so on. The least that should be done is to say that monetary policy should *also* contribute to the fight against unemployment, with the governors of the bank being accountable to governments and parliaments.

The main task however, is the democratization of Europe, based on two principles:

1   Any transfer of power from member states to Europe should *respect the balance of powers*: from national governments to the Brussels executive, and from national parliaments to the European Parliament. When the 'no' campaigners in the French referendum denounced the techno-bureaucratic nature of Europe, they were not berating 'Brussels civil servants' (who are few in number and very committed), but the subterfuge by which national governments used the pretext of negotiating in the intergovernmental context of the Council of Ministers to escape the control of elected representatives, at national or European level.

2   Even if there is democracy on the European level, any transfer of sovereignty upwards to European level will be seen by ordinary citizens as a move away from the sources of power. Any such transfer therefore must be accompanied by transfers downwards towards the local and regional level. Democratic Europe will be a Europe of regions and peoples.

Democracy will be reached by means of the classic method of negotiating a constitution – a basic law – with Parliament performing the constituent function. The major political currents in Europe will put to the electorate their own project for a future Europe; elected representatives of the peoples of Europe, in the European Parliament, will debate and vote, publicly point by point and under the gaze of their electors, on the grand principles and basic rules of a citizens' Europe. Will there be unbelievable squabbling? Of course, as in all constituent bodies. That is what democracy is – the worst system apart from all the others. The Greens in Europe will engage in this battle on a common programme, the one which they have been trying to promote for years in the European Parliament. Let us hope that in the meantime, the squabbling elements of the old Left have been able to agree on a similar programme.

What is the role of the European Parliament in the constitution concocted at Maastricht by governments? Nothing. What can it be, using the weapons it already has from the Single Act – the right to reject the Commission budget and force the resignation of the Commission? It can become the forum for the drawing-up of a constitution, to be put to the people in a referendum.

Sometimes we must have the courage to say 'no' to bring about a world to which we will want to say 'yes'.

PART III

A New Political Force

12

Greens and Others

Ecology as an idea was very quick to win general acclaim in the 1970s, but in France candidates fighting on an ecology platform, and from 1984 onwards the Greens as the political party articulating it on the institutional level, had a tough battle against scorn, condescension, insults and false accusations. Such is the fate of any new movement . . .

Hostility came from a variety of directions. It came from politicians of established progressive movements afraid of competition (the Communist Party in the 1970s, and particularly the Socialist Party in the 1990s). It came from intellectuals rooted in an old progressive culture (classical humanism, or Enlightenment liberalism), who had to cope with a new paradigm which relativizes earlier advances in human consciousness, rather than negating them. There was a general failure to comprehend a new political stance which caused uncertainty about old points of reference (such as Left versus Right) and made people revise their thinking.

This avalanche of criticism was very mixed in nature. Some of it helped ecologists to sharpen their arguments by eliminating the rough edges of their thinking. Other parts were merely the result of bad faith. But the effect of all this criticism from politicians and the media was to bring about a 'rejection of the new' (in this case, ecology) – the characteristic reaction of an established order, typified by rhetorical warnings in the press such as 'our readers may find ecology attractive, but we really must warn them against . . .'

Ecology can only claim cultural hegemony (that is, the ability to refocus public debate around its arguments) when it has dealt with these prejudices. That is the task of this chapter.

All parties nowadays claim to be concerned about the environment. All of them crave ecologists' support, or at least want them to vote for them in the second round of elections. All of them mumble that ecology is too serious a matter to be left to ecologists. But we have seen what little attention they paid to ecology before ecologists became an autonomous political movement.

At the same time, however, the 'modernist' press, and many intellectuals (from the Heidelberg appeal[1] to the regular publication of anti-ecologist tracts, of which the one by Luc Ferry[2] is neither the first nor the last) pursue an assiduous campaign of denigration, accusing Greens once more of being out of touch, racist and all the rest . . .

Resisting false comparisons

This aspect has to be taken seriously. Are the Greens, and more generally political ecology, one of the new political forces in Europe, and the most attractive one for young people, an anti-humanist and racist force, another Le Pen-type movement? The accusation is grotesque: the truth is that the Greens were the only significant political movement to call for voting rights for foreign residents, to support religious freedom for Muslims, to call for work sharing and the cancellation of Third World debt. Nevertheless, false impressions persist.

In France, the refusal of Green candidates to stand down in the second round in several constituencies[3] in order to maximize votes 'against the National Front' angered many people at the end of the 1980s. However, an attempt at this kind of electoral co-operation by left-wing parties had signally failed in the notorious 1983 parliamentary by-election in Dreux, when victory by the National Front candidate marked the first electoral breakthrough by that party. Later, the socialists came round to the Greens' tactics, saying in effect, 'You don't fight the National Front by voting for racketeers, or for other racists.' It is just possible to accuse the Greens of being ultra-left; but they will always say loud and clear that an ecologist could never vote for the National Front. They argue that support for the National Front springs from deep divisions in society, as a result of policies which have been followed over many years. The blackmail of the Socialist Party, the threat of 'us or the National Front', is therefore as counter-productive as was that of the Algerian government ('us or the Islamic Salvation Front'). Disenchanted voters simply remember the corruption of the Socialist Party, despair that the electoral system deprives the Greens of representation and resign themselves to abstaining, though the European elections of 1994 offered the new opportunity of voting for a left-wing populist, Bernard Tapie.

However, the refusal of the European Greens to join the second Gulf War 'crusade of civilization against the Arabs' (as the television journalist Gérard Carreyrou put it) really put the cat among the pigeons. In the face of an anti-war joint stance by Greens, SOS Racisme and dissident communists, the 'Brière affair' offered the opportunity for an anti-Green campaign. (Jacques Brière was a Green representative who used opposition to the second Gulf War as an occasion for an anti-semitist formula. Brière was condemned by the Greens, but the socialist Prime Minister, Michel Rocard, whose government was committed to the war, used the occasion to attack the ecologists: 'Ecology does not in itself establish a blueprint for society, as shown by the curious alliances forged by some ecologist leaders during the Gulf War, or the recent off-beam pronouncements verging on anti-Semitism . . .') Above and beyond the Greens, what is being focused on is political ecology as a blueprint or project for society. And in fact, the main 'ecosophers' (Michel Serres and Félix Guattari) came out against the second Gulf War. It is up to Michel Rocard whether his overall assessment of this human, ecological and political disaster is positive. What did emerge, as far as Greens were concerned, was proof that ecology was not just a matter of protecting small birds!

At this point the anti-ecologist intelligentsia made its appearance, with direct attacks on the Greens' political philosophy. It recognized that they indeed had something to say on humanity and society, and criticized this, or at least selected aspects of it.

An example already referred to several times is Luc Ferry's book *Le Nouvel ordre écologiste*, which gave rise to the kind of operation in the political and media worlds which one has come to expect in France. The problem was in the gulf between the book itself (interesting, and even useful for ecologists) and improper exploitation of it in the media by the author himself and particularly his colleagues who opposed political ecology.

The idea was simple: by defending nature against humanity, political ecology (and especially its radical wing, 'deep ecology') denies human rights, humanism and democracy. In the book, the argument is advanced in a scholarly and circumspect manner. The method is to give a few quotations from writers more or less unknown in France, then to proceed to make false analogies in the same way that Stalinist polemicists attacked 'Hitlero-Trotskyists': 'X quotes Y, or uses the same approach; but Y inspired Z, who is a Nazi. The whole thing is deliberate.' Since there are ecologists who do not always realize some of the possible implications of what they quote, reading Ferry's book can in fact be useful to them . . .

However, the message which appeared in the media was much more simple: 'The Greens are Nazis in the making.' Luc Ferry simply had to refocus on the literal meaning of quotations which in reality were metaphorical or said in jest,[4] to identify in political ecology a reactionary and totalitarian project, while for his own purposes keeping the 'sympathetic' aspects of an ecologist sensibility which up to then nobody knew he shared. Even more directly, a socialist reviewer in the weekly journal *Le Nouvel Observateur* calmly categorized the book as a warning against 'a doctrine which, if taken to its extremes, leads only to fascism or Leftism'. Even more to the point, Michel Winock in the weekly *L'Événement du Jeudi* wrote: 'Anybody who votes for the Greens through love of nature or because of political disillusionment ought to know that they are supporting a new and powerful negation of democracy.' End of applause.

Although readers of this book or of current ecologist writing may not need it to be spelled out, ecologists are humanists as Aristotle was, but they have had 2,400 years to learn that women, or the peoples from whom the Greeks got their slaves, are also part of the human race; and they also say that the paramount responsibility of humanity for nature involves duties to nature, which can properly be called 'the rights of nature'. After all, nobody would try to convince foxes of the rights of chickens.

There is no real need either to spell out another form of anti-ecology, seen in the Heidelberg appeal attacking the influence of ecologists at the Rio Conference. On this occasion, the press did a proper job of investigating an operation mounted by certain industrial lobbies, linked in particular with the German chemical giants. This hymn to 'the alliance of science and industry' in defence of the environment was already laughable, but it became irritating in the context of the contaminated blood affair in France, the dreadful consequence of this famous partnership. But the presence of noted scholars in this appeal should remind us, first, that competence in one area is no guarantee of competence in another – the signatories of the Heidelberg appeal were not consulted for the hundreds of scientific conferences in the run-up to Rio, simply because they were not working in the field; and, second, that a piece of scientific knowledge has no direct consequence for a political position.

Let us go back to the example of the greenhouse effect. There is a scientific consensus on the dangers of increased carbon gases, methane and CFCs in the atmosphere. There is not yet a consensus on the rate of this increase, nor on the geographical spread of its climatic effects. We merely know that there will be effects on the climate, and we try to guess the geostrategic consequences. The precautionary principle therefore demands that we take measures to combat the greenhouse effect. But the strategy to counter the main greenhouse gases (should we prioritize carbon gases or CFCs or methane?) is a matter for political debate, even ethics, and it is moreover rather complex. The pro-nuclear lobby puts the fight against carbon gas at the top of its list, the motor industry puts methane first, Third Worldist ecologists carbon gases, and so on.[5]

Identifying ambiguities

We now come to a discussion of much more fundamental issues. Once it is accepted that political ecology is a critique of a certain modernity, on behalf of values which this modernity ignores, we then need to know whether such an ecosophy can include archaist, ruralist or racist positions. The question is not whether there are ruralist or racist Greens: there are some, as in any other group. A well-argued book by three Green sympathizers, *L'Équivoque écologique*,[6] points to the real problem: ecologists are citizens of the planet, they emphasize the unity of humankind and nature, they are therefore radically anti-racist. They emphasize the *positive* values of community, as against the 'individualist' surge and the deterritorialization which characterizes 'modernity'. However, does not 'community' run counter to 'universality'? And since towns and cities are the places of exchanges, of comings which thumb their noses at the countryside, does not 'community' run counter to urban existence and the development of the individual through myriad encounters in urban settings?

The response of the Greens is that they are for communities characterized by openness and solidarity. They are
against anything which forces people to uproot themselves;
they are for welcoming incomers. They are against the Israeli
bulldozing of centuries-old olive groves, forcing Palestinians
into ghettos in order to settle Russian Jews rejected by
America; they are against anti-Semitic Slavophiles in Russia,
and for the right of Muslims in French towns to have a
mosque. Are these contradictions?

I do not deny that, somewhere along the line from resistance to deterritorialization to rejection of mixing together of
cultures, slippage is possible. Nevertheless, let us consider
raï music, already a culturally mixed music in its Algerian
setting. When it spreads to towns and cities in France, it
becomes part of our cultural heritage, while remaining Arab.
In the festival at the end of the world's NGOs' Ya Wananchi
conference, the reason why both sides of the Atlantic
(Africa, Europe, North and South America) were able to
unite in the music of Mory Konté was that salsa, reggae,
samba and rock recognized a common ancestry in the
rhythms in which members of black African NGOs also
recognized their creation.[7]

What underlies everything is the complex nature of the
relationship of 'each to everyone' to which political ecology
is directed. Communities since antiquity have solved this by
rigid family structures and omnipresent traditions which gave
all their place in a social hierarchy, and at the same time
offered both an individual and collective identity. All knew
what they had to do (and what they could expect of others)
because they all knew who they were and what they were in
relation to others. Conversely, modern individualist society
solves the problem through abstract procedures based on the

anonymity of formally equal individuals – trade relations, wage relations, delegation of power through secret ballot. Paradoxically, the price of this freedom, this formal equality of traders and citizens, is the end of everyone's uniqueness. 'Equality without difference' is the slogan of this abstract universalism, inherited from the eighteenth century and conveyed to the world by the conquering bourgeoisie.

The experience of this transition from ancient, hier-archized, 'holistic' communities to modern, free, equal and individualist societies was (and still is, in the Third World and even rural areas of Europe and the United States) both a liberation and a loss of identity.[8]

Political ecology squares up to the problem of the relationship of each to everyone by trying to safeguard equality *and* difference. How can one remain oneself, be oneself, while living with others and gaining from this relationship with others? This contradiction, as I have said throughout this book, can only be resolved positively if all take on the values of autonomy, solidarity and responsibility, and make them their own, and if democracy develops towards active proposals and participation – a participatory, face-to-face democracy.

A face-to-face democracy presupposes the habit of living together, in other words, a shared territory. If it is true that 'agglomeration is to space what learning is to time – the most immediate form of socialization',[9] then having roots in a territory where people have agreed on something in common is the basis of all socialization, of all true democracy. Better still, it is the starting point for any culture which offers itself to others without ceasing to be itself. It is the starting point for any individual (Ulysses, Joachim du Bellay or Arthur Rimbaud) who goes off all over the world in search of something new. For there to be a meeting, 'the other' has to be accepted as different, as having the material possibility of being and remaining different. At the heart of cosmopolitan urban areas there is an alchemy which creates a new culture out of elements from all over the world; these remain themselves while mingling to form a new mixture. This process, however, does not overturn the truth that the human ecology of Venice, Amsterdam, London or New York is a localized phenomenon, unique and magic, because it is linked to a particular place where 'it all happens', and to nowhere else . . .

If some Greens find it hard to believe that people might want to uproot themselves, or if they prefer a village in the middle of France to Manhattan Village, then so be it – they are entitled to their personal opinion. I myself am one of those ecologists who, sad at the loss of the now demolished Les Halles in central Paris, enthuse over urban centres – Manhattan Village, São Paulo where 'at certain pale hours of the night, one speaks of problems of men, problems of melancholy' (Léo Ferré). Clearly, it is not always easy to reconcile local control of development with openness to the outside world, cultural identity and cultural cross-fertilization, but this is a contradiction arising from the real world (which life and history have always managed to resolve) and not from the Green vision of progress. It is better to debate these issues than berate those who point to the attendant imperatives.

What if the 'ecological ambiguity' was merely the reflection of an *objectively* complex reality? What if the inability of the Greens to 'locate themselves clearly' was an indication that the old frameworks no longer applied? In this case it would be easy to understand how Greens can be anti-racist and not Zionist, anti-Saddam and anti-war, for railways but against some high-speed trains . . .

The Greens: blue, white, red . . . or brown?

It is precisely the absence of a 'clear political stance' for which the Greens are often reproached. By saying they are 'neither Right nor Left',[10] the Greens have been irritating political practitioners and commentators for some time. This is perhaps why they were falsely labelled as extreme Right. We have looked at the bases – both superficial and deep-rooted – of the accusation. We need to examine the reasons expressed by the ecologists themselves.

According to opinion polls, most European Green voters would be happy to see the Right in opposition, while at the same time being extremely dissatisfied with the social and ecological policy of the socialist parties in power. In France, the findings of a major polling organization, and of Jean-Luc Bennhamias and Agnès Roche,[11] are that, apart from minimal traces of right-wing sympathy, Green activists are divided between those 'on the Left' and those 'elsewhere', that is, outside the traditional Right–Left split.

Why then do the Greens not admit to being on the Left? The average activist's reaction is that the socialists represent the execution of Éloi Machoro,[12] the sinking of the *Rainbow Warrior*, being pro-Saddam in the first Gulf War then against him in the second; and that the communists are an authoritarian and pro-nuclear energy party. Here is the first level of explanation – the Greens are not on the Left, because the Left is no longer on the Left. Not very logical, but psychologically understandable. The Greens have taken up the torch of traditional left-wing values (anti-colonialism, disarmament, democracy, anti-racism) and rejected a Left which has abandoned them.

However, there is another level of explanation. Conflict round a Right–Left axis, synonymous with 'order' and 'progress', hardly applies when it is *the direction of 'progress' itself* which is at stake. Clearly, political ecology is radically opposed to certain aspects of a 'progressivism' which has officially united socialist and communist parties in France since the Liberation – progress under the three-pronged head of technology, purchasing power and state influence. Since the Greens are as vehemently opposed to statism as to productivism, they cannot be 'on the Left' if 'the Left' means that kind of progress.

However, it may be argued that this notion of progress, appropriate to the post-war Fordist model of development, is no longer relevant, and that the Socialist Party has dropped the last two 'prongs' in favour of international competitiveness and a free-market approach, nowadays associated with the 'new technological imperative'.

This 'liberal productivism' is just as strongly opposed by ecologists, who base their approach on the negotiated mobilization of human resources, growth of free time, increased solidarity regulated in the context of a welfare community, subordination of the international market to the calm of human communities and the ecological equilibrium of the planet.

Neither at the Left of the former 'Joint Programme for Government'[13] nor in the Left with the mystique of 'modernity', the Greens are suggesting a real alternative to the economic crisis, a different way of moving into the twenty-first century ... without being stifled when they get there. They are the heirs of the emancipation aspirations of humanity, they reject the approach which 'socialism' formerly offered, they reinvent progress. Hence their predicament when they are asked where they are located on a scale which they have moved away from altogether.

In his fine book with the significant title of *Histoire socialiste de la Révolution française*, Jean Jaurès was faced with a similar problem (as E. Labrousse also pointed out in his preface for the edition published by Éditions Sociales): of course the socialists of 1900 were heirs to the emancipation battles of the republicans; but they were no longer part of the monarchy–republic conflict between Whites and Blues. Yet republicans at the time railed at them that 'you have to decide which side you are on.' Gradually, however, socialism managed to redefine the two sides by getting all the rest to locate themselves in relation to its own Red conception of 'progress'.

The ambition of ecologists (and it has had some success) is to assert their conception of progress – a 'Green' one – and force other political movements to locate themselves in relation to it. Of course, a painter like Pissarro would recognize in this green some hints of other colours – the blue of democracy, the red of social concern, libertarian black, the violet of feminism. The Greens, as it were, are green–fuchsia coloured.

Yes, but what about brown – where is their love of the land, of 'living locally'? A case of Maurrassian anti-cosmopolitanism? This is a familiar story. Were not the Reds accused in their time by Blue (republican) liberals of trying to reintroduce a corporatist model of society and of breaking the Le Chapelier Law?[14] The new is often 'a call by a sclerotic tradition for a deeper tradition' (Péguy – the Dreyfusard). Is this the tradition of Le Pen?

The Greens, in common with the National Front, articulate the sigh of a ravaged world, where people are treated as pawns to move around, and attack the old political movements. But that is all. Their final objectives are totally different. The National Front mobilizes pawns against other pawns 'who are overrunning us', whom it accuses of 'polluting our race'. Those accused by the Greens of polluting are those who move pawns around. The Greens' aim is to re-establish solidarities open to new influences, and to help far-off communities to do the same. They are therefore regionalists, pro-Europeans, for immigrants' right to vote, for cancellation of Third World debt. They are against economic emigration (and its causes), but for the integration of immigrants.

Let us be clear about one point: this stance, which on paper is the right one, is in practice liable to all kinds of distortion. There is but a small step, though the Greens refuse to take it, from their slogan 'France's role is not be the nuclear dustbin of Europe' to that of the socialist government of which Brice Lalonde was a member, 'France's role is not to take on the wretched of the world.'

Let me attempt to summarize by using an analogy from geometry. To place all political positions, at any given time, on a single Left–Right (or East–West) continuum is to presuppose that an overarching idea, a new paradigm, is polarizing the concept of progress. On the Left would be put the most radical proponents of 'the new'; on the Right 'reactionaries' (to 'the new'), and in the middle would be moderates. During the French Revolution, 'the new' was democracy; the extreme Left were proponents of direct democracy, the Right of monarchy, and in the Centre were supporters of a restrained democracy. There was thus a move from white to dark blue, with light blue in the middle.

In the twentieth century, social issues are centre stage. On the extreme Left are proponents of a socialist revolution (Reds), on the Right defenders of the interests of property owners, with 'Pinks' in the centre. What about the Blues? Some had become Pink, others occupied the centre Right – they were in favour of democracy, recognizing its social objectives.

The refusal to locate oneself either on the Left or the Right stems from the emergence of a new axis – it could be called North–South – which is superimposed on, and combined with, the existing continuum. The new axis hopes to become the only one on which politics in the future will be located. At one extreme of this axis are 'deep Greens', radical ecologists, who favour a very far-reaching reform of the way we live and produce. At the other extreme are proponents of productivism. And in the centre . . . well, moderate ecologists, those who want to make a small effort provided this does not bring about too great a change.

If this new axis wins the day, people in future will speak of 'left-wing ecology' to describe radical ecologists, whereas nowadays the word 'left' is still associated with 'the Red Left'. 'Left-wing ecologist' nowadays signifies 'an ecologist who does not ignore social issues', as opposed to 'right-wing ecologists' or 'environmentalists', who are not concerned with social issues. In fact, political ecology encompasses social issues. The real conflict within the ecology movement is therefore between the 'deep Greens' (radicals prepared to do a lot both in social matters and for the defence of the environment) and the 'pale Greens' (those prepared to do a bit in both areas).

The fact that there are at present two axes poses tremendous problems for the 'deep Greens' with regard to alliances. Are they closer to the 'deep Reds' or the 'pale Greens'? In the second Gulf War or the anti-Maastricht campaign, they in fact found themselves aligned with some Reds. But on the basic question of which model of development to propound, they are in permanent dialogue with the 'pale Greens'.

The French elections – lessons to be drawn from failure

In 1989 the French Green Party got 10.5 per cent of the vote. At the time, they were the only French ecologist party. Then the socialist minister of the environment, Brice Lalonde, launched a 'pale Green' party, Génération Écologie.

The paradox of the 1992 regional elections was that significant gains by the ecology movement were accompanied by a serious setback for the Greens, who got only 7 per cent of the vote, while Génération Écologie also got 7 per cent. Of the two messages of René Dumont in the early 1970s – that the situation is serious; and that serious steps must be taken – the first one seems now to have been heeded. All parties, even including the most productivist ones, have now taken on a green colouring. Moreover, this phenomenon is worldwide, which is why we had an Earth Summit in Rio. However, the second message is somewhat delayed, which is why the Rio Conference was so disappointing.

It was into this breach between consciousness of danger and the urgent nature of necessary action that Génération Écologie rushed in 1992. It meant that there then was, in France as at world level, a 'pale Green' party – a party for those who said, 'The situation is serious, so there is no point in taking serious measures.' This is like saying, 'Unemployment has reached 3 million, so there is no point in going for widespread work sharing', or 'The atmosphere is getting warmer, so there is no point in suspending the motorway programme', or 'Saving the planet requires a North–South agreement, so why don't we solve conflicts using Patriot and Tomahawk missiles?'

Radical political ecology, which for ten years dominated ecology as a whole (that is, 'the situation is serious' theme), had to fight for hegemony with moderate ecology at a time when everybody was becoming ecologist. It was, I suppose, to be expected, but the Greens could have approached this new state of affairs from a much more favourable position. For example, between 1989 and 1992, they laid the foundation for Brice Lalonde's *coup*, when, from a much less radical stance, he was able to appear more socially conscious, more anti-racist, than them. No doubt it was a question of getting the message over, and a question of tactics – young people, the main chunk of their electorate, were alienated by the Greens' clannishness and the move in the pronouncements of some leaders from 'neither Left nor Right' to 'neither National Front nor democrats'.

To these mistakes by the Greens must be added another element of success for Génération Écologie – the inability of the Socialist Party to recover and transform itself. I had long thought that the Socialist Party would end up by occupying the place of moderates on the Green axis; perhaps this will happen one day. But between 'too deep Greens' and a Socialist Party which had betrayed even the most modest hopes of the Pinks (public morality, for example), there was room for a new party – moderate, pale blue, pale pink and pale green all at the same time.

However, the shock of the regional elections was a lesson for the Greens. Straight afterwards, they recovered from their half-failure to reverse the trend. They had talks with Génération Écologie, and showed both firmness and flexibility in their offer to participate in government (rejecting it at national level, agreeing to it, despite the risks, in the Nord–Pas-de-Calais region). The results were immediate: the media changed their tune over the Greens' programme, Génération Écologie activists rejoined the Greens, and Génération Écologie became more radical in its pronouncements. Even Brice Lalonde admitted that he had not been able to do anything meaningful as a member of the socialist government, and the new Ecologist Alliance of the Greens and GE came out in favour of a thirty-five-hour week with no loss of earnings for the lowest paid.

The decision in the 1993 legislative elections to go for an 'Ecologist Alliance' of the Greens and Génération Écologie rather than align with the Red and Green alternative Left (dissident socialists and communists in the 'Refondation' movement) was in no way a shift to the Right. It represented the strategic option to affirm political ecology as the new basis of hope. Without a strong ecologist pole on the political scene, there is no hope of a massive and deep adherence of Reds to a new conception of progress.

Unfortunately the tremendous victory of the Right in the 1993 national elections created two victims: the Left and the ecologists. The Alliance was weakened by the presence of many 'false ecologist' candidates, and the image of 'false ecologists' provoked a fall in support from the 'people of the Left'. The total ecologist vote was 11 per cent, with 7.5 per cent for the Alliance.

After the defeat, the ecologists became outdated in the media, and Brice Lalonde moved to the Right. The Alliance split, and the two sections were heavily defeated in the European elections of 1994 (3 per cent for the Greens, 2 per cent for Lalonde!). Today French ecologists are trying to reunify around their radical wing, the Greens.

These experiments need to be translated into wisdom. Yes, it is possible to maintain the momentum of the ecologist surge in public opinion in a radical direction – provided the Greens can be both radical and modest. No, ecology does not belong just to them. They are merely, among those who are gradually learning about the imperatives of sustainable de-velopment, the most active and the most conscious of the global scale of problems. They must learn to get together with all ecologists, whatever their previous history, who share this radical approach; they must learn to rally reluctant followers, new recruits, those who dreamed of an effortless ecology; they must learn to isolate opportunists who, in the Greens as well as in other parties, put on Green clothes only to accede to the gold braid of power.

This strategy of gaining power has its rules – the need to be the best proponents of unity, to assume the good faith of other partners, to open hostilities only when it is appropriate and one has the means, to be reasonable in criticism of other partners. This is quite simply ecological politics; it is some-thing which has to be learned ...

At a time when 'Right' and 'Left' are trying to stifle ecol-ogy by reducing it to the 'environment', it is right that the

Greens are affirming the central point above everything: to save the planet and humanity, to get rid of oppression, old injustices and new dangers, we need to question the whole productivist model of development, in its capitalist, bureaucratic and technocratic versions. And we need to do it quickly.

In proposing a new paradigm for life in society, the Greens are hoping for a future role of cultural hegemony. This is the new stage they must reach – transform themselves into a mass movement, open to all those who share their values, whatever their ideological history. The time will eventually come to pose the question of political power – and therefore of alliances with movements which are heirs to long-standing conceptions of progress. But only when they themselves have changed.

13

Political Ecology: The Urgent Task

In the run-up to the twenty-first century, in France as in the rest of the world, the phrase 'tearing apart' crops up all the time to denounce and discredit the present disorder.

The hopes of democratic revolutions have faded. Ballot boxes, when available, are treated with indifference; or else they are banished by warlords with no guiding principles for their nation's future. In France in 1993, there was an uninspiring transfer of power from the fallen heirs of the hopes of the 1970s to a bunch of has-beens who cannot agree on anything. Citizens have simply lost faith in the ability to influence government; the question is whether they still want to govern themselves collectively.

The hope invested in socialism has evaporated. Gone is the dream of a society of producers reconciled through the miraculous nationalization of the means of production. Too many cases of change being usurped have gone so far as to kill the hope of change.

The big contradiction between each and everyone else, regulated by a democracy which once tried to temper market anarchy, is nowadays a yawning emptiness for those excluded from a world not fit to live in. Having no hope of re-establishing social links which have been torn apart, people retreat into something they regard as real, seek solidarity with like-minded people against all those who are in the slightest way different. The rise of corporatisms in France is matched by tribal vendettas in ex-Yugoslavia, Somalia and India.

In a society torn apart, the wind is set fair for racism and fear of 'the other', simply through fear of losing self-recognition. Those who are 'at the bottom of the heap', who used to represent the hope of a redemptive thrust, are nowadays the prime victims of a world shattered to the extent that the comforting relations of wage exploitation are themselves stretched to breaking-point. Comforting? Yes, in the sense that being exploited can be better than being excluded, abandoned, having no sense of belonging . . .

As the twentieth century draws to an end, human beings, who are social animals, no longer know how to live together. In run-down social housing complexes, in industrial regions in terminal decline, in countryside condemned to lie fallow, and, even worse, in countries of Africa or Latin America where the dream of development has turned sour, and, even more dramatic, in those ex-communist countries throwing over a regime which was totalitarian but which allowed everyone a place in society, hatred of 'the other' is fostered by the absence of a common project.

In the 1970s political ecology appeared on the scene with this message: 'Our relationship with nature is bad, because relationships between human beings are already bad.' The old compromises between people were established on the back of nature. Today the gap between humanity and its own living conditions is causing cracks in all the edifices of human civilization. Our development models, formerly unsustainable in the long run, are now falling apart. We are experiencing the crisis of the future.

By treating our environment like a collection of objects at the disposal of our appetites, we have learned to treat other humans as objects. The reason we can no longer put up with our environment is that our lifestyle has destroyed it, but also that the environment is other people, and we can no longer put up with each other. Racism in our towns and cities is hatred of dilapidated communal stairwells, hatred of those who may have caused the dilapidation, hatred of those who live off the dilapidated communal stairwells, hatred of those who may have come from far off (where there are no communal stairwells) to mess up the communal stairwells.

In response to this disaster, this tearing apart, political ecology will only grasp again the torch of hope by showing itself to be what it is: not the guardian of a natural order foreign to humanity, but the promoter of a different way of living together, each with everybody and everybody with nature. To save the planet and guarantee the rights of future generations, we must first work at putting back together today's society – by face-to-face, participatory democracy, putting everybody in the picture while not ignoring opposing interests; by developing the basic values of individual autonomy, solidarity between all, and responsibility for life and for future generations.

The realization of these values will come about in various ways:

- An anti-Taylorian revolution, ending the split between those who direct and those who execute; the negotiated mobilization of human resources to achieve greater efficiency and better-quality products.

- Priority for the fight against accidents and diseases, for ergonomics, waste recycling, and skills which the working community can acquire.
- Priority for growth in free time as an indication of progress and a weapon against unemployment.
- Maintainance of a high level of socialization of income to cover risks in life; recognition of a basic right to income, at the same time reintegrating excluded people into society; this to be done by the development of a socially useful third sector subsidized as unemployment is at present, and offering unemployed people a proper status and reintegration.
- Emphasis on regional development, local government help for business start-up, and local initiatives in the form of technical support, savings schemes and so on.
- Relaunch of a democratic, ecological and social Europe.
- Giving everybody the right to live and work 'locally' by cancelling Third World debt and signing basic co-operation agreements, to help each country to define its own sustainable mode of development.

In all these areas, and all the others one can think of, political ecology is advancing with more modesty than triumphalism. It does not believe in central objectives, in magic solutions, in massive sudden shifts, in the Great Eventide. It does not think that achieving political power will bring a solution: simply that power which is more ecology-oriented will help the effort of each and everybody in civil society.

A friend who is a socio-psychoanalyst, Gérard Mandel, explained that two traps beset those who try to change life. The 'fear of the Father' – the idea that there is nothing we can do, that the system is always against us; and 'wounded narcissism' – the belief that the results of all political actions are insignificant compared with the shining ideal which started us on our quest.

Political ecology, in that it faces squarely the myriad contradictions between each and everybody which go to make up our 'environment', is a perfect illustration of these two traps. Why try to do something when there are billions of people around us conspiring against our environment? And why try to do something when what one achieves is tiny in comparison with what remains to be done?

However, we have merely to reverse the perspective to realize that everybody's environment is every one of us, to understand that it is possible, that it is worth the effort, and that it is of prime importance for everybody to make an effort to change things – to put society back together again, to bring peace to the planet, to reconcile humanity. By an insignificant amount? Yes, but there are billions of us . . .

Political ecology – the modesty of reason, the ambition of will.

Notes

Chapter 1 Ecology without Consciousness is Body without Soul

1 *Le Nouvel ordre écologiste* (Paris, Grasset, 1992). Luc Ferry teaches philosophy at the University of Caen.

Chapter 2 Ecology and Democracy

1 As Francine Comte, author of *Jocaste délivrée* (Paris, La Découverte, 1991) observed, 'The first environment of a person is the mother's womb.'
2 See the fine book by J.-P. Deléage, *Histoire de l'écologie, une science de l'homme et de la nature* (Paris, La Découverte, 1991).
3 This term should not be understood in its narrowly political sense, but as indicating the model of civilization which flourished in northern Europe in the middle of the twentieth century, when workers had not only the right to vote but also the right to social security, rights at work and a right to a share of the fruits of growth.
4 See my chapter entitled 'Une économie à reconstruire', in *Terre, patrimoine commun*, ed. Martine Barrère (Paris, La Découverte, 1992).
5 On the geostrategic aspects of negotiations on climatic change, see my book *Berlin, Baghdad, Rio* (Paris, Quai Voltaire, 1992). In fact, the Rio Conference came down in favour of the South on the atmosphere as well as biodiversity. See ch. 9 below.

Chapter 3　Political Ecology and the Workers' Movement: Similarities and Differences

1 An ecologist and mathematician, whose book *The Ages of Gaia: A Biography of our Living Earth* was published in 1988 (London, Norton).
2 See ch. 1, n. 1.
3 In June 1992, just before the Rio Earth Summit, 264 scientists and intellectuals (of whom fifty-two were Nobel prize winners) launched an appeal, drawn up in Heidelberg, for 'scientific ecology', saying they were concerned about 'the emergence of an irrational ideology opposed to scientific and industrial progress'.
4 According to the concept of the German philosopher Ernst Bloch.
5 These are the sound recommendations of Félix Guattari, sadly missed since his death.

Chapter 4　The Rise and Fall of Economic Liberalism

1 On the crisis of Fordism, and the results stemming from this, see my books *Mirages and Miracles: The Crisis of Global Fordism* (London, Verso, 1988), originally published as *Mirages et miracles* (Paris, La Découverte, 1985), and *Towards a New Economic Order: Post-Fordism, Ecology and Democracy* (Cambridge, Polity Press, 1993), originally published as *Choisir l'audace* (Paris, La Découverte, 1989).
2 This Commission (ECLAC) had a very important role in drawing up the doctrine which made the countries in question temporarily successful, and which provided a model for post-war moves to independence.
3 See my book *Berlin, Baghdad, Rio* (Paris, Quai Voltaire, 1992).

Chapter 5   Ecology as Post-Socialist Economic Logic

1 The *Critique of the Gotha Programme* continues with a critique of another aspect of 'socialism' – its statism. Marx comes out against, for example, state-controlled education; he would have been very surprised by the line-up in the education battles in France in 1984. But that is another story . . .
2 Marx in his work did not ignore this issue: see no. 12 of the journal *Actuel Marx* (1992).
3 The rest of this chapter is essentially a summary of my book *Towards a New Economic Order: Post-Fordism, Ecology and Democracy* (Cambridge, Polity Press, 1993), originally published as *Choisir l'audace* (Paris, La Découverte, 1989).
4 The strange thing is that André Gorz, one of the founders of political ecology in France, abandoned this imperative in his later writing, even though he was a strong advocate of a workers' strategy of this kind to combat 'neo-capitalism'. On this point, he was at odds with the majority of ecologist activists in France.
5 The latest available study on the 'thirty-five-hour' strategy for France is 'Veut-on réduire le chômage?', *Lettre de l'OFCE*, 112 (May 1993), and for Europe as a whole, H. Sterdyniak et al., 'Lutter contre le chômage de masse en Europe', *Observations et diagnostics économiques*, 48 (January 1994).
6 The idea is that on taking power, a majority coalition which included ecologists would immediately legislate for a thirty-five-hour legal working week, with a set number of permitted overtime hours at a higher rate of pay (for example, twice the normal hourly rate), with a part of that rate set aside for the unemployment fund. This would increase in the second year to three times the normal rate, and so on. In this way, firms would not be rushed into change, but would have an increasingly costly period of time to adapt through negotiation. The distribution of productivity gains as free time would become the

norm, and a thirty-hour working week would be reached by the beginning of the next century.

7 *L'Audace ou l'enlisement – sur les politiques économiques de la gauche* (Paris, La Découverte, 1984).

Chapter 6 From Garden to Planet

1 This is another reason why we must not condemn those who seek strictly technical solutions to the imperatives of ecological responsibility, without too brutal a challenge to our comfortable habits. Once again, it is prudent to assume that humankind is not infinitely perfectible.

2 The General Agreement on Tariffs and Trade constitutes the ground rules of international trade. It was renegotiated over many years through the 'Uruguay Round' of talks, the eventual success of which in 1994 allowed it to be transformed into the International Trade Organization.

Chapter 7 A Modest Internationalism

1 The arguments in this chapter were put forward at a session of the Forum of Delphi, which meets regularly and consists of intellectuals and politicians of both North and South. Contributions to the debate appeared in *Ambitions et illusions de la coopération Nord–Sud*, ed. S. Mappa (Paris, L'Harmattan, 1990). I am grateful to members of the Forum, who will recognize in this chapter some of their arguments and criticisms.

2 I am thinking of writers such as Pierre Clastres (*La Société contre l'état*, Paris, Minuit, 1984) and Serge Latouche (*La Planète des naufragés*, Paris, La Découverte, 1991).

3 See, for example, the book by Axelle Kabou, *Et si l'Afrique refusait le développement?* (Paris, Éditions Karthala, 1991).

4 See my book *Mirages and miracles* (London, Verso, 1988).

5 See M. Monimart, *Femmes du Sahel* (Paris, Karthala–OECD, 1989).

6 Lula fought the 1994 Brazilian presidential election campaign on a programme promising to give 800,000 families land over four years at a cost of 10,000 dollars each, using uncultivated land, both public and private. The Workers' Party promised a wealth tax on the richest 150,000 families and a clamp-down on tax evasion, but the need to ensure foreign investment and support from other parties led the Workers' Party to soften its line on privatization and debt. Lula ruled out a moratorium on Brazil's $136 million foreign debt.

Chapter 8   The North–South Divide: Reality or Outmoded Concept?

1 On the points which follow, see my book *Mirages and miracles* (London, Verso, 1988).

2 On these points, see my book *Towards a New Economic Order: Post-Fordism, Ecology and Democracy* (Cambridge, Polity Press, 1993), originally published as *Choisir l'audace* (Paris, La Découverte, 1989).

3 See her book *Debt Boomerang: How the Third World Harms Us All* (Boulder, Colo, Westview Press, 1992).

4 See my book *Berlin, Baghdad, Rio* (Paris, Quai Voltaire, 1992).

Chapter 9   The Rio Conference and New North–South Relations

1 See my book *Berlin, Baghdad, Rio* (Paris, Quai Voltaire, 1992).

2 See S. Goldemberg et al., *Énergie pour un monde durable* (Paris, La Documentation Française, 1992).

3 In *Berlin, Baghdad, Rio*, finished before the Rio Conference, I was still hoping that it would play this role, but I also explained

how the Maastricht Treaty would make this impossible. And that is what happened (see ch. 10 below).

Chapter 10   Pro-Europe Means Anti-Maastricht

1 Interviews with Samuelson and Dahrendorf appeared in the Italian daily *La Repubblica*, 3 September 1992.
2 See *Le Monde*, 6–7 December 1992.
3 See my book *Le Monde enchanté* (Paris, La Découverte/ Maspéro, 1983).
4 See K. Polanyi, *The Great Transformation* (Boston, Beacon Press, 1957).
5 *Libération*, 10 December 1991.
6 Published in 1992 (Paris, Quai Voltaire).
7 *Le Monde*, 17 July 1992.
8 *Libération*, 28 July 1992.

Chapter 12   Greens and Others

1 See ch. 3, n. 3.
2 See ch. 1, n. 1.
3 Elections for the National Assembly are held on a two-round single-constituency system. To qualify for the second round, a candidate needs 12.5 per cent of the first-round vote, but has the option of withdrawing to maximize support for the better-placed candidate of another left- or right-wing party.
4 Typical of this is his interview, published on 10 December 1992, with a journalist from *Les Clés de l'Actualité*, which has a readership particularly among adolescents. In it he said, apparently seriously, that 'certain ecologists in the United States and France are proposing the physical elimination of 350,000 people a day.' He pretends not to know that the notion of 'right of nature' is merely a metaphor for 'duty of humans in respect of

nature', a metaphor made necessary, as he explained in his book, by the peculiarities of common law in English-speaking countries. On the contrary, in France and countries with administrative law, the notion of 'right of nature' is useless since there exists a 'duty of the state to protect nature'.

5　The book by an activist of the ecologist association Bulle Bleue, Yves Lenoir, *La Vérité sur l'effet de serre – le dossier d'une manipulation planétaire* (Paris, La Découverte, 1992), is a fine example of the possible turning to anti-ecologist use of internal debates within ecology. Obsessed by the use made of the greenhouse effect by supporters of nuclear energy, Yves Lenoir, starting from an accurate critique of certain models of carbon gas remanence in the atmosphere, manages to deny the dangers of carbon gas, and comes down on the side of those who say, 'Why not just let it happen?' Given the power and success of this position up to now, his critique of a ghostly 'climate lobby' seems insignificant . . .

6　P. Alphandery, P. Bitoun and Y. Dupont, *L'Équivoque écologique* (Paris, La Découverte, 1991). From this book, which is way above the much less informed, much less penetrating and much more malevolent book by Luc Ferry, the media picked out only one page (p. 127), which summarily denounced Antoine Waechter's alleged 'neo-Pétainist neo-ruralism'.

7　Conversely, non-Westernized Asians felt excluded from this music.

8　See Louis Dumont, *Homo aequalis* (Paris, Gallimard, 1985).

9　G. Benko and A. Lipietz, *Les Régions qui gagnent* (Paris, PUF, 1992).

10　That was the official stance of the French Green Party when the Left was in power. Since then, like other Green parties in Right-dominated Europe, they more easily accept a left-wing label.

11　See Jean-Luc Bennhamias and Agnès Roche, *Des Verts de toutes les couleurs* (Paris, Albin Michel, 1992).

12 Leader of the New Caledonia independence movement, who was killed by police under a French socialist government.
13 In 1972, the Socialist Party, the Communist Party and the smaller Movement of Left Radicals signed a 'Joint Programme for Government' in anticipation of taking power in France. By the time this happened in 1981, the updating attempted in order to take account of the world economic crisis had failed, and in any case the inter-party co-operation on which the programme was based had virtually disappeared; there were communist ministers in Mauroy's government 1981–3, but this government had a socialist majority in the National Assembly and had no need of communist support.
14 Le Chapelier was a deputy who in 1791 proposed a law forbidding the 'coalition' of people in the same job or profession to promote common interests and protect rights.

Index

Index compiled by Ann Barham